I0013389

PUBLISHER COMMENTARY

Military Handbooks have been developed from an evaluation of facilities in the shore establishment, from surveys of the availability of new materials and construction methods, and from selection of the best design practices of the Naval Facilities Engineering Command (NAVFACENGCOM), other Government agencies, and the private sector. This handbook was prepared using, to the maximum extent feasible, national professional society, association, and institute standards. Deviations from these criteria in the planning, engineering, design, and construction of Naval shore facilities cannot be made without prior approval. Design cannot remain static any more than can the naval functions it serves or the technologies it uses. Accordingly, recommendations for improvement are encouraged.

Unfortunately, few Military Handbooks address the need for cybersecurity to prevent cyber-physical attacks against government facilities. Many of the building controls in military installations are old and being replaced with state-of-the-art building controls, however many new devices were not designed to be "connected" and very little thought was given to secure them from cyber-attack. Recent events have clearly demonstrated the need to secure everything from web cams to electrical utility grids.

Each copy of the MIL HNDBKs we publish includes a list of cybersecurity publications produced by the National Institute of Standards and Technology (NIST) as well as Unified Facilities Criteria (UFC) that are directly applicable to the topic for consideration during the planning process. These publications cover a wide range of cybersecurity concepts that are carefully designed to work together to produce a holistic approach to cybersecurity primarily for government agencies and constitute the best practices used by industry. This holistic strategy to cybersecurity covers the gamut of security subjects from development of secure encryption standards for communication and storage of information while at rest to how best to recover from a cyber-attack.

Why buy a book you can download for free?

Some documents are only distributed only in electronic media.

We at 4th Watch Books are former government employees, so we know how government employees actually use the standards. When a new standard is released, an engineer prints it out, punches holes and puts it in a 3-ring binder. While this is not a big deal for a 5 or 10-page document, many UFC documents are over 100 pages and printing a large document is a time-consuming effort. Unfortunately, reductions in government over the years means that now the engineer himself has to print his own copy (no one has a secretary anymore). So, an engineer that's paid $75 an hour is spending hours simply printing out the tools he needs to do his job. That's time that could be better spent doing engineering.

4th Watch Books prints these documents so engineers can focus on what they were hired to do – engineering. This is important because there are not as many engineers working in government as there used to be, so wasted time on clerical duties is unproductive.

If you are paid more than $10 an hour and use an ink jet printer, buying this book will save you money. It's much more cost-effective to just order the latest version from Amazon.com

Luis Ayala, Publisher, 4th Watch Books

List of Applicable NIST Publications:

UFC 4-010-06	Cybersecurity of Facility-Related Control Systems
NIST SP 800-82	Guide to Industrial Control Systems (ICS) Security
Whitepaper	NIST Framework for Improving Critical Infrastructure Cybersecurity
NISTIR 8170	The Cybersecurity Framework
FC 4-141-05N	Navy and Marine Corps Industrial Control Systems Monitoring Stations
UFC 3-430-11	Boiler Control Systems
NISTIR 8089	An Industrial Control System Cybersecurity Performance Testbed
UFC 1-200-02	High-Performance and Sustainable Building Requirements
NIST SP 800-12	An Introduction to Information Security
NIST SP 800-18	Developing Security Plans for Federal Information Systems
NIST SP 800-31	Intrusion Detection Systems
NIST SP 800-34	Contingency Planning Guide for Federal Information Systems
NIST SP 800-35	Guide to Information Technology Security Services
NIST SP 800-39	Managing Information Security Risk
NIST SP 800-40	Guide to Enterprise Patch Management Technologies
NIST SP 800-41	Guidelines on Firewalls and Firewall Policy
NIST SP 800-44	Guidelines on Securing Public Web Servers
NIST SP 800-47	Security Guide for Interconnecting Information Technology Systems
NIST SP 800-48	Guide to Securing Legacy IEEE 802.11 Wireless Networks
NIST SP 800-53A	Assessing Security and Privacy Controls
NIST SP 800-61	Computer Security Incident Handling Guide
NIST SP 800-77	Guide to IPsec VPNs
NIST SP 800-83	Guide to Malware Incident Prevention and Handling for Desktops and Laptops
NIST SP 800-92	Guide to Computer Security Log Management
NIST SP 800-94	Guide to Intrusion Detection and Prevention Systems (IDPS)
NIST SP 800-97	Establishing Wireless Robust Security Networks: A Guide to IEEE 802.11i
NIST SP 800-137	Information Security Continuous Monitoring (ISCM)
NIST SP 800-160	Systems Security Engineering
NIST SP 800-171	Protecting Controlled Unclassified Information in Nonfederal Systems
NIST SP 1800-7	Situational Awareness for Electric Utilities
NISTIR 7628	Guidelines for Smart Grid Cybersecurity

Copyright © 2017 Luis Ayala All Rights Reserved

MIL-HDBK-1012/1
15 MAY 1989
SUPERSEDING
DM-12.1
APRIL 1983

MILITARY HANDBOOK

ELECTRONIC FACILITIES ENGINEERING

AMSC N/A

DISTRIBUTION STATEMENT A. APPROVED FOR PUBLIC RELEASE: DISTRIBUTION IS UNLIMITED

AREA FACR

THIS PAGE INTENTIONALLY LEFT BLANK

ABSTRACT

This military handbook presents design criteria for Category Codes 131 and 132, communication facilities, antennas, and transmission lines. The contents cover general engineering requirements, as well as specific requirements for the major types of electronic facilities, including automatic data processing centers and transportables. The design criteria are intended for use by experienced architects and engineers.

THIS PAGE INTENTIONALLY LEFT BLANK

FOREWORD

This handbook has been developed from an evaluation of facilities in the shore establishment, from surveys of the availability of new materials and construction methods, and from selection of the best design practices of the Naval Facilities Engineering Command (NAVFACENGCOM), other Government agencies, and the private sector. This handbook was prepared using, to the maximum extent feasible, national professional society, association, and institute standards. Deviations from these criteria in the planning, engineering, design, and construction of Naval shore facilities cannot be made without prior approval of NAVFACENGCOM HQ (Code 04).

Design cannot remain static any more than can the naval functions it serves or the technologies it uses. Accordingly, recommendations for improvement are encouraged and should be furnished to Commanding Officer, Chesapeake Division, Naval Facilities Engineering Command, Code 406C, Washington, DC 20374-2121. Telephone (202) 433-3314.

THIS HANDBOOK SHALL NOT BE USED AS A REFERENCE DOCUMENT FOR PROCUREMENT OF FACILITIES CONSTRUCTION. IT IS TO BE USED IN THE PURCHASE OF FACILITIES ENGINEERING STUDIES AND DESIGN (FINAL PLANS, SPECIFICATIONS, AND COST ESTIMATES). DO NOT REFERENCE IT IN MILITARY OR FEDERAL SPECIFICATIONS OR OTHER PROCUREMENT DOCUMENTS.

ELECTRONIC FACILITIES CRITERIA MANUALS

Criteria Manual	Title	PA
MIL-HDBK-1012/1	Electronic Facilities Engineering	CHESDIVCHESDIV
DM-12.02	High Altitude Electromagnetic Pulse Protection for Ground-Based Facilities	

ELECTRONIC FACILITIES ENGINEERING

CONTENTS

FIGURES

TABLES

Section 1: INTRODUCTION

1.1   Scope. This military handbook, MIL-HDBK-1012/1, establishes criteria for the design of electronic facilities.

1.2   Cancellation. This handbook, MIL-HDBK-1012/1, cancels and supersedes DM-12.1, dated April 1983.

1.3   Responsibilities. The design of Navy electronic facilities requires close coordination between the designer and other parties. Responsibilities involved in design stages are as follows:

1.3.1   Chief of Naval Operations (CNO). The CNO is the Director of Naval Communications, who sponsors and supports Naval communication facilities. through the Naval Telecommunications Command and other commands. The CNO, as the user, states the needs of the operating and supporting facilities for research and development, improved equipment, new equipment, spare and repair parts, consumables, training, maintenance, personnel facilities, and any other requirements of the user. In many instances, the CNO is responsible for supporting the Defense Communication Agency (DCA), which is the sponsor for the nation's world-wide Defense Communications System (DCS).

1.3.2   Naval Facilities Engineering Command (NAVFAC). NAVFAC is responsible for design, development, and construction of the facilities ancillary to and/or required for the support or housing of electronic equipment and operating personnel. NAVFAC provides technical guidance and direction in shore facility engineering from project inception to completion.

1.3.3   Space and Naval Warfare Systems Command (SPAWAR). SPAWAR exercises technical control of design, development, procurement, and installation of the electronic equipment for an electronic facility at a shore activity. SPAWAR provides technical guidance and direction in shore electronic engineering from project inception to completion, except in special cases where the electronic systems or equipment is specifically assigned to another command.

1.3.4   Maintenance Authority. SPAWAR exercises technical control through regional and district offices, whose responsibilities include installation and maintenance engineering of electronic equipment that is beyond the capacity of station forces. Regional and district offices represent SPAWAR for electronic engineering control while the architect-engineer develops the design.

1.3.5   Designer. The architect-engineer or equivalent Navy personnel (hereafter called "the designer") usually enters design development after the operational requirement has been established and before actual construction begins. The designer plans the building to satisfy the operational requirements normally set forth in the Base Electronic System Engineering Plan (BESEP) (refer to paragraph 1.5.1) and prepares project drawings and specifications under the control of NAVFAC and the guidance of SPAWAR. Requirements for military construction and special projects that do not directly involve electronic equipment, and thus do not require a BESEP, are

1

identified in project documentation, The designer must maintain close liaison with the NAVFAC command responsible for the particular project, which will coordinate all technical matters with the sponsors and users of the project.

1.4   Policy. The design of electronic facilities should be based on operational requirements. The primary consideration is that operational communication buildings and other electronic facilities be sited, arranged, and constructed to provide the most effective communications possible. Whenever compromises between operational requirements and convenience, cost, or energy conservation become necessary, such compromises should be resolved in favor of operational requirements. Where there is conflict between two mandatory Government documents, the more stringent requirement governs. In all cases, the BESEP shall be the overriding document.

1.5   Principal Data Sources

1.5.1   BESEP. The basic document used by SPAWAR for planning and controlling shore station electronic installation work is the BESEP. It translates operational requirements into a detailed technical plan for meeting the requirements. It is prepared by representatives of SPAWAR, in collaboration with NAVFAC, and is approved by the sponsor for use in design development. A detailed description of the BESEP, as well as policy and procedures for its use, is given in NAVELEXINST 11000.1, The Base Electronic System Engineering Plan (BESEP): Policy and Procedures for Utilization of, dated 21 July 1971. The BESEP generally provides the following information:

1.5.1.1   General Requirements. The BESEP establishes the requirements of the project, the scope and layout of the planned facility, the design and installation of the electronic system, information on the electronic equipment to be used, details of system checkout, and characteristics of the physical plant.

1.5.1.2   Design Data. The BESEP includes information on structural limitations; recommended locations of electronic equipment, power panelboards, special red or black panelboard designations, and special power requirements; identification of red areas; antenna locations and the number, type, performance, and frequency ranges required; cable types and termination locations; Radio-Frequency (RF) shielding requirements, other requirements for precautions against radiation hazards, and characteristics of the source of radiation; high-altitude electromagnetic (HEMP) pulse protection requirement; electronic equipment areas of concentrated heat load and requirements for special air conditioning or environmental control; recommended locations of compressed air outlets, specifying pressure and valve requirements; grounding systems; and internal security. Requirements relevant to the specific site and supporting facilities are also included. The completeness of such information and the amount of detail furnished to the designer depend on the circumstances of the project, and, in emergencies, may be brief and subject to augmentation as the project progresses.

Section 2:   SITE CONSIDERATIONS

2.1   Suitability of the Site.   The primary consideration in selecting a site is its technical adequacy for meeting performance objectives. Generally, these objectives are maximum signal-to-noise ratios at the receivers and maximum effective power radiated in the desired direction from the transmitters. Although other factors enter into selection of a site, compromises for the sake of economy or logistic convenience must not interfere with performance. The principal considerations for technical adequacy are radio-frequency noise and topography, but suitability for construction at reasonable cost, link requirements between components of the communication station, land costs, and logistic support requirements are also considered. Other factors are availability of utilities, climate, foundation stability, survivability, physical security, and expansion potential.

2.2   Relationship to Design.   The designer does not select the site, but the considerations leading to its selection must be understood and incorporated in the design. Before the designer begins work, the Field Technical Authority of SPAWAR, in cooperation with the Engineering Field Division of NAVFAC, conducts a site selection survey and an Electromagnetic Compatibility (EMC) evaluation as part of the preparation of the BESEP.

2.2.1   Site Selection Survey.   Considerations related to the electromagnetic and physical environments that influence selection of a site are listed in NAVELEX 0101,114, NAVELEX Calibration Program. A sample site selection survey checklist is included in the appendix to that manual.

2.2.2   Electromagnetic Compatibility (EMC) Evaluation.   Any factor that prevents or degrades the reception of signals also degrades the ability of the site to perform its mission. The receiving and direction-finding site should be located where signal reception is known to be good. The EMC evaluation, described in NAVELEX 0101,106, Electromagnetic Compatibility and Electromagnetic Radiation Hazards, identifies environmental electromagnetic interference from all sources, as well as radio noise. The EMC evaluation is the responsibility of SPAWAR. All pertinent information will be set forth in the BESEP.

2.3   Isolation.   Optimum radio communications depend largely on isolation of the site from sources of interference and on proper dispersion of structures within the site, Minimum separation distances for electromagnetic interference protection of receiver sites are given in NAVELEX 0101,102, Naval Communications Station Design, and in Table 1. Special separation requirements for Naval Security Group (NAVSECGRU) receivers are given in NAVELEX 0101,108, Naval Security Group Elements, Design and Performance. Specific requirements for each project are developed in the BESEP; variations required by local conditions are also established by the BESEP or by authorized changes to it.

Table 1
Separations and Clearances

FACILITY	SOURCE OF INTERFERENCE[1]	MINIMUM DISTANCE
Radio receiver (R) station[2]	High-power transmitter stations: Very low, frequency	25 mi (40 km)
	Low frequency/high frequency	15 mi (24 km)
	Other transmitter stations not under Navy control[3]	5 mi (8 km)
	Airfields and glide paths: For general communications	5 mi (8 km)
	For aeronautical receiving at air stations	1,500 ft (457 m)
	Teletype and other electromechanical systems: Installed in shielded room or level signaling and keying modified	No requirement
	Installed in unshielded rooms or high level signaling and keying operation:	
	Large installation (communication center)	2 mi (3.2 km) from nearest antenna
	Small installation (1 to 6 instruments)	200 ft (61 m) from nearest antenna
	Main highways	3,000 ft (914 m)
	High-tension overhead power-lines-receiver station feeders	1,000 ft (305 m) from nearest antenna
	Habitable areas (beyond limits of restriction)	1 mi (1.6 km)
	Areas capable of industrialization (beyond limits of restriction) Light industry) Heavy industry)	3 mi (4.8 km) 5 mi (8 km)
	Radar installation (depending on type)	1,500 ft (457 m)
Radio transmitter (T) stations	Other transmitter stations	3 mi (4.8 km)
	Airfields and glide paths: For general communications transmitting	3 mi (4.8 km)
	For aerological transmitting at air stations	1,500 ft (457 m)
	Main highways	1,000 ft (305 m)
	High-tension overhead power lines	1,000 ft (305 m) from nearest antenna

Table 1 (Continued)
Separations and Clearances

FACILITY	SOURCE OF INTERFERENCE[1]	'MINIMUM DISTANCE
Direction finder **(DF) stations (other than** Wullenweber type)	Elevated horizontal conductors[4]	Must not subtend a vertical angle exceeding **3°** at base of DF antenna
	Railroads	1/4 mi (0.4 km) from antenna
	Rivers and streams	No effect
	Radio transmitter stations: Major Minor or emergency	10 mi (16 km) 1 mi (1.6 km)
	Housing areas	1,500 ft (457 m) from DF site
	Ambient interference	Less than 3uV/meter throughout desired frequency range
Communications centers and terminal equipment building	Communication center should conform to the minimum separations from Receiver Station as given above	- - -
Control link facilities	Separation between RF building and antennas	Max distance 300 ft (91 m)
	Separation between RF building and operations building	Max distance 1,500 ft (457 m)

'Tabulated sources interference apply to DF stations of any frequency. For additional sources applicable to specific frequencies refer to Handbook of Naval Shore Station Electronics Criteria, NAVELEX 0101, Appendix VIII.

[2]Maximum distance between transmitter and receiver stations is only limited by microwave path and logistics. For the majority of applications this distance should be limited to 30 miles (48 km).

[3]The following NAVELEX requirements also govern distances to non-Navy transmitter stations:
   a) Signal from non-Navy station shall not exceed 10 microvolts per meter (field intensity) at the Navy site boundary.
   b) Harmonic or spurious radiation from the non-Navy station shall not exceed 5 microvolts per meter (field intensity) at the Navy site boundary.

[4]If conducting towers are used, or if the horizontal conductor is a receiving antenna, refer to NAVELEX 0101, Appendix VIII.

2.3.1   Buffer Zones. Requirements for buffer zones, which protect the site and adjoining communities from man-made radio noise, are described in NAVELEX 0101,102, Radio Communications Station Design. Registry of this land under local or state laws that restrict further development of radiation-sensitive areas is the most desirable means of protecting the site.

2.3.2   Other Considerations. Because of electromagnetic hazards or security considerations, it may be desirable to isolate buildings from community facilities, population centers, and public transportation lines. If hazardous conditions are absent, however, proximity to transportation and to community recreation facilities can be desirable.

2.4   Expansion. Provide for future expansion as required by the BESEP. If there are no specific requirements, plan for expansion as a matter of course. Locate support facilities near the boundary of the station to permit expansion without undue invasion of the antenna area. When the budget permits, construction of separate structures or self-contained elements is preferred to expansion by extension of existing facilities.

2.5   Siting Procedure. Developing the optimum site configuration requires coordination of civil engineering and electronic engineering. The designer will be provided with preliminary site layouts developed by the electronic system engineering activity. These documents show the site's dimensions, schematic building layout, utility requirements, access road layout, direction and number of transmission paths, size and layout of supporting structures, and special design considerations for optimum performance of the electronic system.

2.6   Site Plan Components. Using the preliminary site layout prepared by the electronic system engineering activity, information from the site survey, and the criteria herein, the designer shall prepare a final site plan. In addition to the location of facility components, the final plan shall show the site boundary and property lines; the base line and bench marks; access roads and parking areas; elevation, azimuth, and coordinates for the center of each antenna; underground utilities; underground services; and existing buildings and facilities. In general, electronic facilities (structures) are similar to other Navy shore facilities, and the criteria in the NAVFAC design manuals are applicable. Characteristics of specific electronic buildings and site components are discussed in Section 8. Special considerations for physical security and personnel safety are discussed in Sections 6 and 7. Site development criteria unique to shore electronic facilities are discussed below.

2.7   Survey Base Line. The construction base line normally is established by the siting survey performed by the electronic system engineering activity. Special precautions are required to protect the base line markers from movement or loss during construction.

2.8   Layout. The general location of buildings is established on the general development map of an activity. Technical details bearing on the location and orientation of buildings are given in the BESEP and furnished to the designer for adaptation to the site. The arrangement of facilities at a communication station varies according to mission. The functions of each facility, as discussed in Section 8, should be considered in planning the layout. Detailed siting criteria for specific electronics facilities may be found in the appropriate Naval Shore Electronics Criteria Manual, 0101 Series. Antenna spacing and siting, which usually receive first consideration, are discussed in NAVELEX 0101,104, HF Radio Antenna Systems; the locations of buildings are determined in relation to the antenna locations.

Operating buildings, such as transmitter and receiver buildings, and the terminal point of transmission lines should be as near the center of the station or antenna field as possible. Support buildings should be near the station boundary. Where radio interference is a problem, locate roads and parking areas so that traffic will not interfere with reception at receiver stations. Insofar as operating and security requirements permit, buildings should be oriented to provide maximum economy in heating and cooling and to keep paving to a minimum. Figure 1 is a schematic representation of a typical major communication station system.

2.9   Site Security Considerations. Facility layouts must be compatible with an overall installation security plan and must consider the location of guard posts, patrols, and security response forces; the location and characteristics of intrusion detection systems; facility access control; and natural factors. Security factors that influence exterior layouts are discussed in MIL-HDBK-1013/1, Design Guide Lines for Physical Security of Fixed Land-Based Facilities. Security at electronic facilities is discussed in greater detail in Section 6.

2.10   Surface and Subsurface Drainage. The requirements of NAVFAC DM-5.03, Drainage Systems, shall apply, except as follows:

2.10.1   Runoff. Calculation of storm water runoff shall be based on a storm with a 50-year design frequency.

2.10.2   Pipes. Metallic pipe and reinforced concrete pipe are inappropriate at some sites. Their use will be determined by project requirements.

2.10.3   Drainage. Swale drainage shall be used to the greatest extent possible. Minimal design velocities shall be maintained to avoid damage of ground planes.

2.10.4   Exceptions. Storm drain pipe shall not be used through an antenna ground plane.

2.11   Paved Areas. The requirements of NAVFAC DM-5.5, General Provisions and Geometric Design for Roads, Streets, Walks, and Open Storage Areas, shall govern, except as follows:

2.11.1   Traffic Areas. Parking areas, pedestrian walks, and other traffic areas adjacent to buildings shall be surfaced with bituminous concrete or portland cement concrete.

2.11.2   Roads. Access roads shall be all-weather roads, with surface courses adequate for design traffic loads.

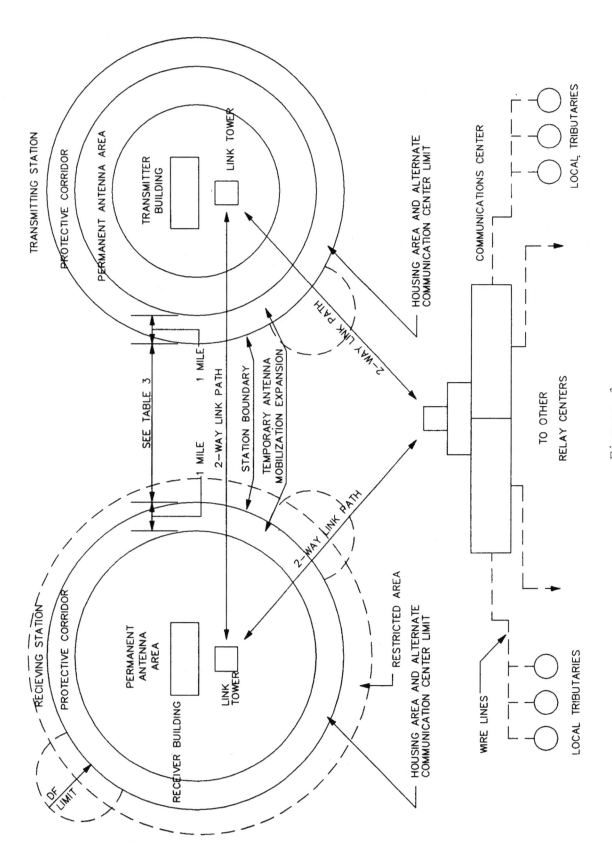

Figure 1
Typical Major Communication Station.

2.11.3   <u>Curbs</u>. Curb and gutter normally are not provided.

2.11.4   <u>Guardrails</u>. Guardrail shall be provided where required for personnel safety or for protection of equipment. The requirements of OSHA Standard 29 CFR 1910.23, <u>Standards for General Industry</u>, shall apply.

2.12   <u>Water Supply and Wastewater Disposal</u>. The requirements of NAVFAC MIL-HDBK-1005/7, <u>Water Supply Systems</u>, and MIL-HDBK-1005/8, <u>Domestic Wastewater Control</u>, shall apply, except as follows:

2.12.1   <u>Water Supply</u>. Hauling water is not an acceptable means of supplying water to a permanent electronic facility site.

2.12.2   <u>Pipe.</u> Where metallic pipe and reinforced concrete pipe are inappropriate at a particular site, this will be indicated in the project BESEP.

2.12.3   <u>Lawn Irrigation</u>. Lawn irrigation normally is not provided.

2.12.4   <u>Fire Protection</u>. In electronic facilities of noncombustible construction, water demands and hydrant spacing for external fire protection shall be determined in accordance with the requirements of MIL-HDBK-1008, <u>Fire Protection Engineering</u>, for unsprinklered facilities under light-hazard, favorable conditions. For combustible construction, other guidelines in MIL-HDBK-1008 shall apply.

2.12.5   <u>Conformance to Regulations</u>. Water supply and wastewater disposal systems shall conform to applicable local, state, and federal requirements and regulations.

2.13   <u>Landscaping and Ground Cover</u>. The requirements of MIL-HDBK-1013/1 shall apply, except as follows:

2.13.1   <u>Placement</u>. Landscaping and ground cover shall be provided only to the extent that they reduce site maintenance. Vegetation shall not interfere with antennas and ground mats. Some site areas must be kept free of vegetation; the designer shall consult the electronic system engineering activity for this information.

2.13.2   <u>Fire Breaks</u>. Where buildings are of combustible construction, fire breaks shall be provided in accordance with MIL-HDBK-1008. Fire break requirements within the antenna field shall be based on the specific exposure hazards.

2.14   <u>Fencing, Gates, and Guard Towers</u>. The requirements of DM-5.12, <u>Fencing, Gates, and Guard Towers</u>, shall govern, except as specified otherwise in Section 6 of this handbook.

THIS PAGE INTENTIONALLY LEFT BLANK

Section 3:   ARCHITECTURAL AND STRUCTURAL ENGINEERING

3.1   Basic Construction Criteria

3.1.1   General Requirements. Permanent communication buildings shall be windowless structures of masonry and/or concrete providing open space free of columns and similar obstructions. Buildings housing electronic equipment shall be of noncombustible construction. Where practicable, operating spaces should be designed for resistance to blast, earthquakes, hurricanes, and typhoons. In overseas locations, locally available materials and methods shall be used wherever possible.

3.1.2   Equipment Spaces. Emergency generators should be located in separate buildings, although they may be located within the operations building if they are properly isolated from the rest of the structure in terms of fire protection, sound attenuation, and vibration control. Battery rooms, consisting of cells mounted on manufacturer-supplied battery racks, are normally adjacent to the uninterruptible power supply equipment room. The battery room should be windowless, adequately ventilated to prevent explosive concentrations of hydrogen gas, reasonably well insulated against thermal heat loss and heat gain, and located to minimize solar heat gain.

Frequency conversion equipment should be as close as possible to the equipment it serves. Motor generators should be located in a separate room to reduce noise levels and heat gains in operating spaces. Static converters may be located in the equipment space or operating space, because they produce minimal heat and noise. Operating spaces containing electronic equipment usually require close temperature and humidity control. Vapor barriers beneath floor slabs and incorporated into roofing are usually sufficient to prevent moisture migration into and out of interior electronic equipment spaces. Additional protection must be provided where exterior walls form part of the equipment space.

3.1.3   Special Requirements. Special requirements, such as special finishes, gaskets, or thermally isolated glazing, will be specified by the BESEP. In some facilities, special equipment and operating characteristics may require that the wall be constructed of nonferrous and nonmagnetic materials. This requirement will be stated in the BESEP. Bonding and grounding for control of compromising emanations shall be in accordance with NACSIM 5203, Guidelines for Facility Design and Red/Black Installations. Shielded enclosures shall conform to the requirements of NAVFAC NFGS-13093, Radio Frequency Shielded Enclosures. Demountable Type, and NFGS-13094, Radio Frequency Shielded Enclosures. Welded Type. Shielding, as specified in the BESEP, shall be incorporated into the design of the structure, and its installation shall be scheduled at a time in the construction phase when it can be done most economically.

3.2   Structural Design

3.2.1   Foundations. Foundations design shall conform to the criteria in NAVFAC DM-7.02, Foundations and Earth Structures.

3.2.2   Framing. Structural framing shall conform to the criteria in
NAVFAC DM-2 series Structural Engineering. Roof framing shall be designed to
support all roof-mounted equipment.

3.3   Exterior Walls. Unless otherwise specified, walls shall be masonry
units, or, for certain buildings, precast or cast-in-place concrete. Wall
construction shall be consistent with the requirements of NAVFAC DM-1.01,
Basic Architectural Requirements & Design Considerations.

3.4   Interior Walls

3.4.1   Permanent Partitions. Interior partitions for stairwells, vaults,
elevator hoistways, toilets, and other areas requiring fixed partitions shall
be masonry units or concrete. Partitions in storage areas shall be of
concrete masonry.

3.4.2   Nonpermanent Partitions. Interior partitions in electronic
operating spaces shall be nonload-bearing and removable. Electrical power and
control wiring shall not be located in these partitions. Permanent partitions
separating electronic operating spaces from other spaces shall be fire rated
and constructed in accordance with National Fire Protection Agency (NFPA) 75,
Computer/Data Processing Equipment. All partitions using metal framing and/or
surfacing shall be suitably bonded and grounded, if required by SPAWAR.

3.5   Floors

3.5.1   Permanent Floors. Selection of floor construction should take into
consideration the placement of cables and wiring for electronic equipment. An
equipotential plane conforming to MIL-HDBK-419, Volume 1, Grounding. Bonding,
and Shielding for Electronic Equipment and Facilities, Basic Theory,
and Volume 2, Grounding, Bonding, and Shielding for Electronic Equipment and
Facilities Applications, shall be installed in the floor of all spaces. The
preferred method of placing cables and wiring is given in the BESEP for the
facility.

3.5.2   Raised Floors. When raised flooring is required, it shall conform
to the requirements of NFPA 75, MIL-F-29046, Flooring, Raised: General
Specifications for, and MIL-HDBK-1008. The flooring system shall be either a
bolted grid (stringer) or a rigid grid system, as required by the BESEP.
Finishes shall be seamless vinyl or laminated plastic. All air supply panels
and similar inserts shall be flush with the flooring surface. Installation
shall conform to MIL-HDBK-419, Volumes 1 and 2. A raised floor installation
over a level permanent floor is generally preferable for flexibility of cable
access and routing; however, depending on the facility layout, a dropped or
recessed permanent floor may be used.

3.6   Roofs. Roofs shall be constructed of noncombustible materials.
Where HEMP pulse requirements must be considered, metal roof deck is
preferred; elsewhere, precast or cast-in-place concrete is preferred. All
roof construction shall conform to the requirements of MIL-HDBK-1190, Facility
Planning and Design Guide, and MIL-HDBK-1008.

3.7   Ceilings. Ceiling design shall be consistent with requirements for lighting, air conditioning, ventilation, cable tray layout, acoustical treatment, and fire protection, as specified in the BESEP. Where raised floors are used, 8 feet (2.44 meters(m)) is the minimum clear height above the raised floor, and 10 feet (3.05 m) is preferred. In uninterruptible power supply, transmitter, and similar equipment spaces where heat dissipation is a design factor, a clear height of more than 10 feet (3.05 m) may be required.

3.8   Finishes. Flame spread and smoke developed ratings for interior finishes shall conform to MIL-HDBK-1008.

3.8.1   Operating Areas Housing Electronic Equipment. Floors shall be 1/8-inch vinyl tile with a vinyl or rubber tile base. Walls shall be acoustic panels. Ceilings in operational electronic spaces shall also be acoustic panels.

3.8.2   Storage Spaces, Vaults, and Mechanical Equipment Rooms. Floors shall be concrete with a dusted-on finish with hardener; floor hardener must be used on all concrete floors in buildings housing electronic equipment. In general, bases should not be used. Where required for protection of wall finishes or for sanitation, however, vinyl or rubber bases shall be used. Walls shall be exposed. Ceilings shall be of exposed concrete or noncombustible, suspended construction.

3.8.3   Offices, Corridors, and Toilets. Finishes shall be as specified in MIL-HDBK-1001/2, Materials and Building Components.

3.8.4   Other Spaces. In uninterruptible power supply spaces and emergency generator rooms, floors shall be concrete with a dusted-on finish with hardener. Bases shall not be used. In battery rooms, floors and bases shall have an acid-resistant finish. Walls and ceilings shall be exposed.

Section 4: MECHANICAL ENGINEERING

4.1   General. All mechanical criteria that apply to naval facilities in general also apply to electronic facilities. Only items specifically applicable to electronic facilities are covered in this section.

4.2   Heating, Ventilating, and Air Conditioning (HVAC) Systems

4.2.1   Outside Design Conditions

4.2.1.1   Permanent and Transportable/Nonrelocatable Facilities. NAVFAC P-89, Engineering Weather Data, shall be used to determine winter and summer outdoor design conditions. HVAC systems for spaces designated as critical by the BESEP shall be designed on the basis of the 99 percent column for heating and the 1 percent dry-bulb and mean coincident wet-bulb columns for ventilating and air conditioning. Design of systems for other spaces shall be based on the 97.5 percent and 2.5 percent columns, respectively.

4.2.1.2   Transportable/Tactical and Transportable/Relocatable Facilities. If the location of the installation is known and it is probable that the location will not change, the outdoor design conditions defined above shall be used. If the location is not known, or if it is probable that the container will be relocated, HVAC equipment shall be designed for the "worst case" likely to be encountered. Temperature and humidity extremes are defined in MIL-STD-210, Climatic Extremes for Military Equipment.

4.2.2   Inside Design Conditions. Spaces not containing electronic equipment but meeting the programming priority requirements of MIL-HDBK-1190 shall be air conditioned. Inside design conditions shall be in accordance with NAVFAC DM-3.03, Heating, Ventilating, Air Conditioning and Dehumidification Systems. Spaces not meeting the priority requirements shall be heated and ventilated only, also in accordance with NAVFAC DM-3.03. Requirements for electronic equipment spaces are discussed below. In all cases, the BESEP should be consulted for specific guidance.

4.2.2.1   Computer Rooms. These areas generally should be maintained at 72 ± 2 degrees Fahrenheit (F) (22 ± 1 degrees Celsius (C)), 45 ± 5 percent relative humidity (RH) year-round. If a wider range in space conditions can be tolerated by the equipment, the less restrictive values should be used.

4.2.2.2   Receiver Buildings and Similar Areas. Electronic equipment in receiver buildings, telephone and switchgear rooms, radio direction-finder facilities, and similar areas generally require a year-round environment of 75 ±5 degrees F (24 ±2 degrees C), 50 ± 5 percent RH.

4.2.2.3   Transmitter Buildings. Depending on the type of system utilized to remove waste heat from the facility (see Section 8), the following conditions apply:

a) Ventilated spaces, such as plenums, 90 degrees F (32 degrees C) minimum, 5 degrees F (3 degrees C) over ambient maximum and relative humidity as naturally occurs with the related ventilation.

b) Air conditioned spaces, such as operating corridors and control rooms, 80 +/- 5 degrees F (27 +/- 2 degrees C) and 50 +/- 10 percent relative humidity.

c) Heat exchange/air conditioned spaces, such as transmitter rooms that are not partitioned into separate corridors and plenums, 70 degrees F (21 degrees C) minimum and 90 degrees F (32 degrees C) maximum with 60 percent maximum relative humidity. Such facilities may have, but are not required to have separately enclosed control rooms conditioned as in para. 4.2.2.3 b, above.

4.2.2.4   Uninterruptible Power Supply (UPS) Equipment Rooms. Depending on the type of system utilized to remove waste heat from the room (refer to Section 8), the following conditions apply:

a) Ventilated equipment rooms are controlled to the same temperature conditions as in para. 4.2.2.3 a, above, for ventilated transmitter spaces.

b) Heat exchange/ventilation (similar to para. 4.2.2.3 c, above), except using ventilation as the auxiliary heat removal means (in lieu of air conditioning) can also be used, in which case the environmental limits should be 70 degrees F (21 degrees C) minimum, 5 degrees F (2 degrees C) over ambient maximum with relative humidity as naturally occurs with this system.

c) Air conditioning 80 +/- 5 degrees F (27 +/- 2 degrees C) and 50 +/- 10 percent relative humidity during normal operation with conditions rising but not exceeding 120 degrees F (49 degrees C) and relative humidity as will occur during a 15 minute power outage. Note that this will require a thermal inertia system in most installations.

d) For the systems described in paras. 4.2.2.4 a, b, and c, if other heating is not available, a unit heater shall be installed in the equipment room to provide heating when the UPS is off for extended maintenance periods (no waste heat available) and to prevent condensation damage. For these occasions the heater shall maintain, and the controlling thermostat shall be set for, a temperature of 85 degrees F (29 degrees C). Unit to be energized only when the UPS is off to avoid cross control.

4.2.2.5   UPS and Microwave Equipment Battery Rooms. These rooms shall be ventilated at all times. During cold weather, sufficient heat shall be provided to remain within the following limits:

a) Temperature - 65 degrees F (18 degrees C) minimum, winter only from waste heat, and a maximum as naturally occurs with ventilation.

b) Humidity - No minimum and 90 percent maximum. See para. 4.2.2.4 d) for method to limit.

c) A unit heater shall be installed in the battery room to provide heat when waste heat is not available, to augment waste heat if inadequate and to prevent condensation. The heater shall maintain, and the controlling thermostat shall be set for 60 degrees F (16 degrees C). This heater shall be be energized during winter only via a summer/winter switch in series with the control thermostat. Humidity shall be limited to 90 percent by energizing the unit heater at any time without the limitation of the summer/winter switch but with the limitation of a differential temperature limit thermostat set for 5 degrees F (3 degrees C) over the outside ambient temperature.

4.2.2.6   Emergency Generator Rooms. Refer NAVFAC DM-3 Series Mechanical Engineering, for interior design requirements.

4.2.2.7   Transportables. Inside conditions for transportables are the same as for permanent facilities depending on the needs of the equipment therein as outlined in the BESEP. This includes temperature limits and humidity high limit. Humidification is normally not provided unless a water supply is available.

4.2.3   Guidelines for HVAC System Design. In addition to the specific requirements in the BESEP, the following guidelines apply to all projects.

4.2.3.1   Simplicity. Naval electronic facilities are located worldwide, often in harsh environments. In many locations maintenance is a problem because of the lack of skilled labor and the difficulty in obtaining spare parts. Systems that are straightforward in concept and design are preferred to complicated systems that are difficult to operate and maintain.

4.2.3.2   Equipment Selection. NAVFAC DM-3.03 provides information applicable to a variety of system designs. The following should be noted however:

   a) Sensible-to-total-heat ratios. Electronic facilities differ greatly from comfort cooling applications. The cooling load in electronic equipment spaces is predominantly sensible; sensible-to-total-heat ratios approaching one are common. Cooling coils designed for comfort applications are inappropriate since they excessively dehumidify equipment spaces to satisfy the sensible load. Conversely, air handlers serving electronic equipment spaces should not serve comfort-cooled areas as well, since they may not satisfy the latent load in those areas.

   b) Fan-coil units. NAVFAC DM-3.03 notes that fan-coil units should not be used for comfort cooling in humid climate zones. Properly designed, however, they are suitable for electronic equipment spaces. Vapor barrier protection should be adequate and outside ventilation air should be minimized.

   c) Economizer cycle. NAVFAC DM-3.03 restricts the use of economizer cycle controls, mainly in relation to the economics of operation. For electronic equipment areas, however, economizer cycles make precise control of humidity difficult. For those applications where no backup cooling is provided, an economizer cycle does offer a valid means of emergency cooling, even in warm climates, if no other means are available.

4.2.3.3   Fuel Selection. In electronic facilities, cooling or waste heat removal is the predominant mode of operation and heating requirements may be nonexistent or minimal. For those applications where additional heating is needed on an occasional basis only, when equipment is off or when unseasonable weather exists, electric resistance heating should be considered because of its low first cost, low maintenance, simplicity, and reliability. If a fuel selection analysis is prepared for areas not containing electronic equipment, life-cycle costing techniques should be in accordance with NAVFAC P-442, Economic Analysis Handbook.

4.2.3.4   Humidification. Electronic equipment areas generally require less humidification per thousand BTU per hour (MBH) of heating than comfort applications.   Humidification needs are higher if a proper vapor barrier is not provided, if excessive fresh air is admitted to the space, if dehumidification during the cooling process is excessive, or if the humidity ratio of the outside ventilation air is less than the humidity ratio desired. The following methods of humidification are suitable:

a) Steam grid. This method is the simplest and provides the quickest response. It is preferred when steam (devoid of chemicals) is available. This process will add to the cooling load.

b) Atomized water. Atomized water provided by air-assist, mechanical, or water spray methods provides fast response and reduces the cooling load.   It requires in-line demineralizers to avoid mineral dust in the air, however, this can be expensive if the water is high in mineral content (hard) or if large quantities of outside ventilating air are admitted.

c) Evaporative. Humidification, by pan-type humidifiers, gives a slow response, possible overshoot and may add to the cooling load. Maintenance requirements are high in areas with hard water although an automatic flush cycle helps to reduce maintenance.

d) Steam injection. Steam injection by electric package units provides medium to fast response, requires large amounts of electrical power and adds to the cooling load. Scaling problems are the same as with the evaporative pan method.

4.2.3.5   Dehumidification. Electronic equipment areas also require less dehumidification per ton of cooling than comfort applications. Less dehumidification is required in properly designed electronic facilities. Cooling coils, therefore, should be designed for higher sensible-to-total load ratios. Occasional higher latent loads can be handled by small separate dehumidifiers located in the space and controlled by a humidistat if necessary. Reheat should be avoided where possible and, if required, should utilize waste heat.

4.2.3.6   Air Distribution. Where floors are raised, underfloor distribution of conditioned supply air is convenient. Unless the equipment is specifically designed to receive raw supply air, direct connection between the air plenum and the equipment should be avoided. Instead, relocatable floor panels should supply air to the room and the equipment should take tempered air from the room. If overhead distribution is provided, low-velocity/low-pressure duct-work is desirable. Both with overhead and underfloor air distribution, air terminal devices must be located to allow the air to reach the area of the loads. If the electronic equipment is in a high-bay area with an overhead cable grid network, and if the outlets are located above the network, the air may tend to short circuit. When the cable is under the floor, poor air distribution may also occur due to cables or cable troughs blocking the limited under floor space. Extending the supply or return ducts to floor level at columns and walls should be considered in high-load or congested areas.

4.2.3.7   Air Filtration. All outside and recirculated air shall be filtered. Replaceable media or filters are preferred in lieu of cleanable filters because of their lower manpower requirements. Where filtration is a problem (as in dusty locations), prefilters of lower efficiency can be used in conjunction with higher efficiency filters to extend their life. All filter banks should have permanently installed indicators to give a warning when pressure drop exceeds the maximum recommended. Roll filters should be controlled by an adjustable timer (first choice) or a static pressure controller (second choice); however, note that static pressure controllers are sometimes upset by the action of dampers and other occurrences resulting in a waste of filter media. Table 2 shows the recommended minimum filter performance as specified in American Society of Heating, Refrigerating and Air Conditioning Engineers (ASHRAE) Test Standard 52-76, Method of Testing Air-Cleaning Devices used in General Ventilation for Removing Particulate Matter.

Table 2
Minimum Filter Performance
(% Efficency)

ELECTRONIC EQUIPMENT AREAS	PERCENT
Equipment rooms requiring near clean room conditions	60
Telephone switchgear, computer rooms and relay rooms	45
UPS rooms and transmitter spaces	40
All other, in general (see BESEP)	30

AREAS NOT CONTAINING ELECTRONIC EQUIPMENT	
Air conditioned spaces	20
Spaces without air conditioning	15
Pre Filters (when used)	20
Roughing Filters (when used)	15

4.2.3.8   Energy Conservation. Operating economy and energy conservation are highly desirable but these goals are secondary to the reliability of the system for electronic facilities. Where energy monitoring and control systems are already in existence or are scheduled for installation, consider their use for monitoring only (not control) to insure the HVAC system is not increased at the expense of reliability. Use the following guidelines.

a) Base minimum outside ventilation air flow rate for air conditioned areas on average expected building occupancy rather than on a simple percentage of total air circulated. Where occupancy will vary considerably, an O_2 ‹ or CO_2 sensor system to control the outside fresh air damper should be considered for keeping outside air ventilation rates at the minimum required level.

b) Avoid conflict between components within the systems, such as excessive latent cooling that must be offset with humidification during temperature control or excessive sensible cooling that must be offset with reheat during humidity control. System designs that properly match the sensible-to-total load ratio performance of the equipment to that of the application are necessary.

c) Avoid conflict or cross-control between units when multiple units are used, as in computer rooms with multiple units.

d) Use capacity increments for improved part-load performance.

e) Features such as economizer cycles (except when provided and used only as emergency ventilation), night setback and wide-throttling-range or dual-setpoint thermostats are incompatible with electronic equipment spaces that require close control.

f) For areas not containing electronic equipment, use proper zoning to permit economizers, night setback and other energy conservation options.

g) Use simple but adequate controls. Electric controls are more than adequate for most applications and are simple to understand and easy to maintain by station forces. Electronic controls are more complicated and sometimes subject to error due to the proximity of heavy currents or RF interference. Although the trend is toward more sophisticated electronic type controls, consideration should be given to the fact that outside contract maintenance would probably be needed to maintain them. Pneumatic controls require a compressor, dehydrator and space for same in the mechanical room. Unless constant and proper maintenance is given this type system it may become contaminated with moisture and will be erratic in operation thereafter. This type system is not recommended.

4.2.4   Applications.   For spaces not containing electronic equipment, the requirements of NAVFAC DM-3.03 shall apply. Requirements for specific electronic facilities are described in Section 8. Requirements which apply to more than one facility type are described herein.

4.2.4.1   Computer Rooms and Spaces with Similar Equipment.   Specific requirements for computer rooms, receiver rooms, telephone and switchgear rooms, and electronic equipment maintenance shops will be indicated in the

BESEP. If the manufacturer's recommended conditions differ from those specified by this manual or the BESEP, the matter should be referred to SPAWAR and NAVFAC for resolution.

a) Specialized equipment. HVAC units specifically designed for computer rooms and similar cooling applications are sometimes referred to as process coolers. They generally differ from units designed for comfort cooling, in that the cooling coils are designed for a much higher sensible-to-total cooling ratio; discharge air relative humidity may be limited to about 80 percent, as opposed to nearly 100 percent in comfort cooling applications; and the cubic feet per minute (CFM)-per-ton value may be as high as 600 to 800, as opposed to 400 for comfort cooling. These units are designed for year-round use rather than the 1000 to 3000 hours of operation of comfort air conditioners. Both in-room equipment and central systems must be tailored to the needs of the spaces served. This includes providing the proper degree of air filtration, adequate humidification capability, the ability to provide cooling in cold weather, and the proper type of cooling coils.

b) System types. HVAC equipment for electronic equipment/computer room areas may be of the following types:

(1) Direct expansion, glycol- orwater-cooled;

(2) Direct expansion, air-cooled;

(3) Central chilled water system with in-room air units;

(4) Central chilled water system with central air handlers;

(5) Process chillers (for direct water-cooled computer equipment).

Advantages and disadvantages are discussed in the ASHRAE Handbook Series and in Section 8 of this manual. In general, systems with glycol are quite popular due to the simplicity of installation and ease in maintaining winter operation. However, it should be noted that these type systems are the least efficient of all systems when evaluated on a BTU/watt power use basis.

c) Provisions for standby. The preferred approach is to divide the total required capacity into increments of reasonable size and then provide one or more extra increments/units for backup. With central systems, consider configuring piping and ductwork to allow systems serving noncritical areas to serve critical areas in an emergency. On the water side, multiple chillers, pumps and cooling tower cells should be provided where applicable. Consult the BESEP for guidance in regard to areas requiring backup HVAC equipment.

d) Auxiliary equipment. Areas requiring close temperature and humidity control year-round shall be provided with 7-day temperature and relative humidity recorders. Alarms should indicate out-of-tolerance room temperature and relative humidity and appropriate HVAC equipment off-line or off-normal conditions.

4.2.4.2 UPS Equipment Rooms. Figure 2 shows several approaches for the environmental control of these areas. These methods are also applicable for transmitter buildings, except that transmitter buildings do not require backup heating and ventilation.

a) Fans. Provide two fans capable of handling the amount of air exhausted through the equipment cabinet plus about ten percent for good sweep at the hood. Fans shall operate with one on the utility circuit and the other on the UPS circuit. The system shall be designed to ensure continuous operation of either fan. Note that the UPS must be sized to carry this additional fan load in addition to its technical load.

For the parallel arrangement, the primary fan shall be connected to the UPS circuit and the standby fan to the utility circuit. Normal operation shall be with the primary fan only operating via manual start, and automatic start of the backup fan in the event of failure of the primary fan. Both fans shall be equipped with sail switches to operate the failure alarm.

For the series arrangement, both fans shall operate during normal operation via manual start, and failure of either must be sensed by a differential static pressure switch across each fan to operate the failure alarm.

Both fans in the series configuration shall be of the non-overloading type, such as those having backward inclined air-foil blades and a fairly shallow static pressure versus CFM performance curve, where CFM is plotted as the ordinate, so that a loss of one fan will not drastically reduce the cooling air flow. The parallel arrangement requires more space than the series arrangement. Ducting for the parallel arrangement must be split so it is more complicated and low-leakage backdraft dampers must be provided to prevent short-circuiting. Therefore, the series arrangement is the preferred arrangement. The supply fan plus return fan arrangement is a series arrangement in the sense that failure of either fan would still provide ventilation.

b) Hoods. Hoods shall be provided over the UPS exhaust ports to prevent waste heat from spilling into the equipment room. This will limit room temperature to the supply air (outside air) temperature except for insignificant gains in the summer. In the winter air temperature will be limited to a value determined by the room thermostat setting. Hoods should be approximately 6 inches (152.4 mm) larger all around than the ventilating discharge and should extend to within 18 +/- 6 inches (457.2 +/- 152.4 mm) of the discharge port. Refer to the ASHRAE Handbook Series for a detailed discussion of exhaust hood design. If space for hoods is not available, an alternate means should be designed to minimize spillover of exhaust air into room air.

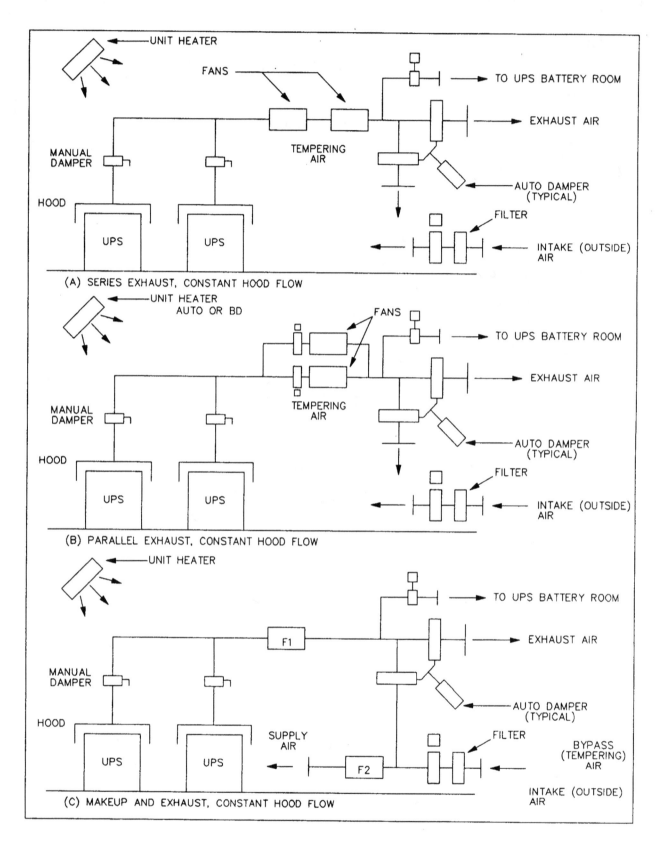

Figure 2
UPS Equipment Room Ventilation Schemes

c) Ductwork and controls. Exhaust ducts should be routed to a location that will minimize mixing of exhaust and makeup air. Modulating dampers should be of the low-leakage type, and controls should be arranged to, maintain the specified temperature by modulating exhaust, return, and intake air dampers in response to the room thermostat. Dampers should fail to the maximum outside air (safe) position. Ducting should be arranged so that return (tempering) air is thoroughly mixed with the supply air to give a uniform room temperature devoid of raw air drafts. This is even more important in colder climates. A firestat shall stop the fans on a high-temperature alarm signal; note that the firestat must sense room temperature or, if of the duct-mounted type, must be set at an appropriate value over the normal hot air exhaust temperature. Smoke detectors, if provided, shall be provided in accordance with NFPA 90A, <u>Standard for the Installation of Air Conditioning and Ventilation Sys</u>tems.

d) Other arrangements. When variations in the illustrated schemes are necessary, the design should provide the same degree of reliability and performance. Automatic duty switching of normal and standby fans in the parallel arrangement is not recommended on the basis of limited benefit versus additional complexity that reduces reliability. One such variation is where the UPS cannot be ventilated due to the inaccessability to outside air, outside air quality or outside air temperature. For these applications, a chilled water air handler tied either to a dedicated small chiller or to the central system can be used. However, since the chiller will stop when the outage occurs, a thermal inertia ride-through tank must also be supplied along with a small circulating pump to supply the air handler during the outage. The UPS must supply power to both the air handler and the small pump motor for the inertia tank in addition to its normal load.

Figures 3 and 4 show examples of thermal inertia designs. The degree of reliability required and the space available will dictate whether dualization of the air handlers and chillers in these applications is necessary. Caution is advised on the use of other air conditioning arrangements that do not have a thermal inertia capability to ride through a 15 minute outage since the UPS must continue to operate for 15 minutes when an outage occurs. During this period waste heat must continue to be removed from the equipment room or the temperature in the average sized room will rise to the over-ambient cut out point as sensed by the UPS safety thermostat at which point it will preserve itself by stopping and the load will be dropped. UPS environmental control systems or components subject to failure must be dualized in order to meet the uninterruptible requirements of the system. Lack of ride through capability will preclude use of D-X air conditioning systems even if dualized. Chilled water systems augmented with chilled water storage tanks for ride through can be utilized when necessary.

e) Auxiliary heating. UPS equipment rooms require backup heat whenever the equipment is down for maintenance or repair. Electric resistance heaters are normally preferred, since usage is minimal. The heaters should be sized to maintain a minimum of 60 degrees F (16 degrees C) in the space with the UPS equipment off (winter), and 90 degrees F (32 degrees C) (summer) to remain above the highest likely dewpoint, with the ventilation equipment de-energized.

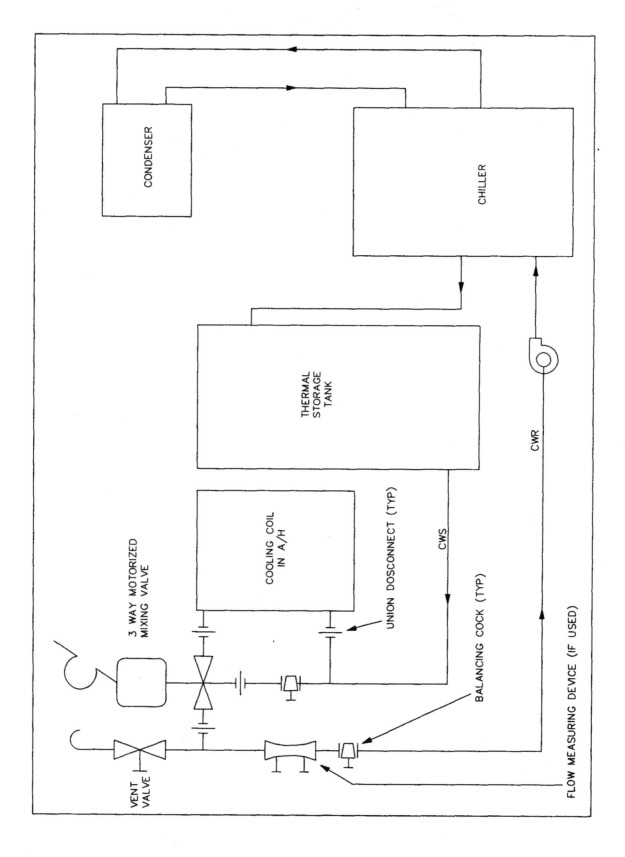

Figure 3
Thermal Inertia System for Individual Chilled Water to Cool UPS

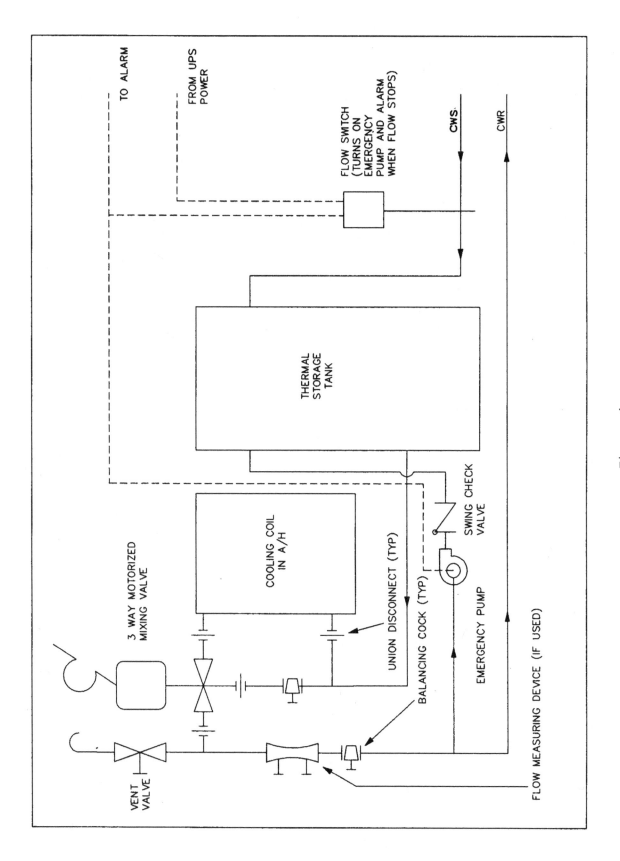

Figure 4

Thermal Inertia System for Central Chilled Water to Cool UPS

4.2.4.3   UPS Battery Rooms. The most important environmental control system requirement of the battery room is to keep the battery electrolyte within an acceptable range of temperature. Normally, this can be done by heating and ventilation only. Ventilation is also necessary to limit hydrogen accumulation within the room. Batteries used with UPS equipment give off negligible heat and low volumes of hydrogen gas when being charged. The high thermal inertia of the battery electrolyte causes its temperature to float between the daily ambient temperature extremes; therefore, acceptable electrolyte temperatures can be maintained by heating and ventilating, even though the ventilated room temperature may approximate the outside ambient temperature.

a)   Ventilation. The ventilation rate required is dependent upon the hydrogen evolution rate which, in turn, depends on the type, size, temperature, charging rate, and number of cells in the battery bank. Hydrogen gas evolution is highest during the last hours of an equalizing charge when most of the batteries will be fully charged and the charging energy is simply hydrolizing the electrolyte. During this period and at 760 millimeters (mm) of mercury absolute atmospheric pressure, one cell will release hydrogen at the rate of 0.016 cubic feet per hour (ft^3/h) of hydrogen for each ampere of charging current flowing.

One fully charged lead calcium cell, with 1.215 specific gravity electrolyte, at 77 degrees F (25 degrees C) temperature, will pass 0.24 amperes of charging current for every 100 ampere-hour cell capacity (measured at the eight-hour rate), when subject to an equalizing potential of 2.33 volts. This current will double/halve for each 15 degrees F (8 degrees C) rise/fall in temperature.

The required capacity of a cell (ampere-hours at the eight-hour rate) and the number of cells for a given UPS application depends on the UPS size, design and operating time. Where several UPS and battery brands are available, a variety of combinations are possible.

To calculate the required rate of ventilation for the battery bank of a 750KVA Emerson UPS (for example), consisting of 182 GNB Inc. cells, type PDQ-27, each having a nominal 1360 AH capacity at the eight-hour rate and being equalized at an electrolyte temperature of 92 degrees F (33 degrees C), proceed as follows:

EQUATION: Hydrogen Rate (HR) = $\dfrac{0.016}{60}$ x 0.24 x 2 x $\dfrac{1360}{100}$ x 182 = 0.317 CFM   (1)

Where:

> 0.016 = hydrogen emission rate per cell per ampere charge (ft^3/h)
>
> 60 = number of minutes per hour
>
> 0.24 = charging current per 100 AH cell capacity at 77 degrees F (ampere)
>
> 2 = doubling factor for 15 degrees F (8 degrees C) rise in electrolyte temperature (above the normal 77 degrees F (25 degrees C))
>
> 1360 = capacity of one cell at the eight-hour rate (ampere-hour)
>
> 100 = increment of cell capacity that will pass 0.24 ampere current charge (ampere-hour)
>
> 182 = number of cells

Concentrations of hydrogen below four percent are not flammable. To meet the Occupational Safety and Health Act (OSHA) requirements, limit hydrogen concentration to one percent. The required ventilation rate is:

EQUATION: Ventilation Rate (VR) = $\dfrac{0.317 \; CFM}{0.01}$ = 31.7 CFM   (2)

Notice that this is a small volume. Other factors, such as, lighting, other equipment and solar-thermal gains, will require additional ventilation. Therefore, a ventilating rate of no less than 400 CFM should be considered. To provide redundancy, use two fans, each sized for half the flow. Fans may be wall-mounted, roof-mounted, or ducted in-line. Makeup air shall be filtered as previously specified. A schematic of the heating and ventilating scheme is shown in Figure 5. Fans shall be on the utility power circuit.

b) Heating. The preferred method of heating UPS battery rooms is a simple ducted arrangement using waste heat from the UPS equipment. Backup heat would then be required only when the UPS equipment is down for maintenance or repair. Electric resistance unit heaters are preferred, because of low first cost maintenance and utilization. The heater should be on the utility power circuit.

c) Controls. In the scheme depicted in Figure 5, the modulating damper should be controlled in winter by a wall-mounted thermostat, set at 65 degrees F (18 degrees C). A switch should make it possible to bypass the thermostat in the summer to fully close the damper in the branch duct from the UPS equipment exhaust irrespective of temperature to take full advantage of daily range and to obtain a lower electrolyte temperature within the specified range. Dampers should be of the low-leakage type. Fans should run continuously, except when de-energized by the firestat. Fan failure alarms and hydrogen gas buildup alarms are not required. Fans should, however, be

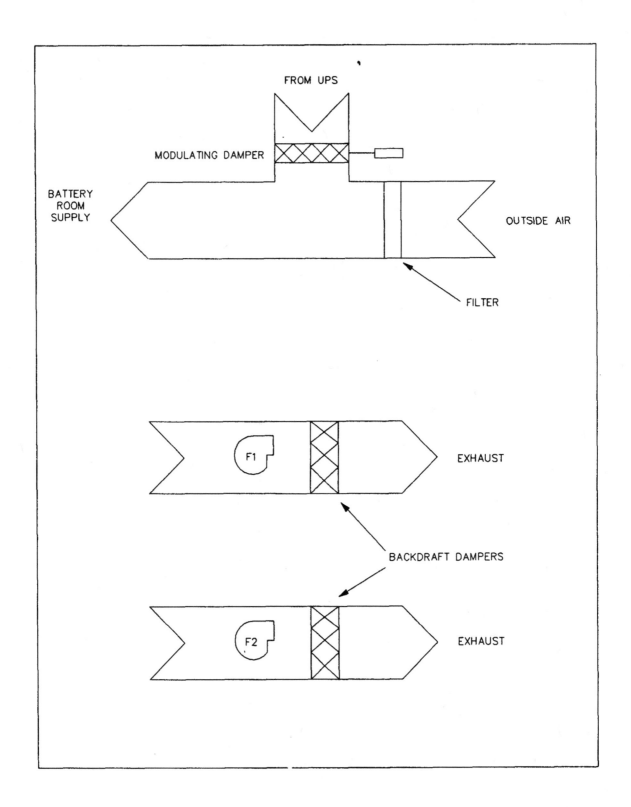

Figure 5
UPS Battery Room Scheme

observed daily to insure they are both operating. If the fans are of a type making observation difficult, then a failure alarm should be considered

d) Safety features. Battery rooms shall comply with OSHA regulation 1926.403, Battery Rooms and Battery Charging.

4.2.4.4   Shielded Enclosures. HVAC systems for areas that require electrical and/or acoustical shielding should be one of two types:

a) Electrically shielded enclosures. For these areas, supply and return ducts penetrating the shield shall be provided with radio-frequency (RF) cutoff cores at the penetration points. Temperature and humidity control sensors shall be located in the return air duct outside the enclosure rather than the space itself to avoid filters in the control wiring. Requirements for backup, inside design temperatures and similar factors shall be as indicated in the BESEP for the specific facility type.

b) Electrical/acoustical shielded enclosure. Air handlers within the room should be considered to avoid large supply and return ducting. Minimum sized fresh air supply/exhaust openings or ducts will still be necessary and must have RF cutoff cores and acoustic attenuators. Temperature and humidity controls can then be within the room and control wires need not penetrate the shield. This method requires only that power for the fan, plus a few watts for control, penetrate the shield, and therefore limits the power that must be filtered. The air handler in the room may use direct expansion, chilled water, steam or hot water coils supplied via piping from remote heating and cooling units. The advantage is that main power for these functions need not enter the room, eliminating the need to filter it. The piping penetrating the shield must be metallic, must be bonded to the shield, and must be long enough to ensure RF cutoff.

4.3   Plumbing. Plumbing systems shall be in accordance with NAVFAC DM-3.01, Plumbing Systems. Special requirements not covered by DM-3.01 are as follows:

4.3.1   Battery Rooms. UPS battery rooms and other spaces containing electrolytic solution must be provided with emergency showers and eye wash facilities, as specified in OSHA 1926.403, Battery Rooms and Battery Charging.

4.3.2   Shielded Enclosures. Domestic water and other plumbing piping penetrating the shield must be bonded to it to ensure RF cutoff.

4.3.3   Transportables. Generally, the requirements of DM-3.01 do not apply to the tactical type of transportable.

4.4   Fire Protection. Design of fire protection and signaling systems is covered by MIL-HDBK-1008 and MIL-HDBK-1190. Fire protection signaling systems are briefly discussed in Section 5 of this handbook. The following discussion is intended only to highlight data contained in the reference documents which should be consulted for more detailed guidance.

4.4.1   Areas Not Containing Electronic Equipment. Offices, classrooms and similar spaces are usually sprinklered, especially if the building is of combustible construction, or if large amounts of combustible material are contained in the space. Most of these areas will be classified as light hazard but some, such as auditoriums and classrooms, may be classified as ordinary hazard. Wet-pipe sprinkler systems are normally required.

4.4.2   Electronic Equipment Areas. The classification of the hazard depends on the type of equipment in the space and its other contents. The degree of fire protection required depends on the value of the equipment and its importance to the mission of the facility. Incidental electronic gear of comparatively small value does not require special treatment. Essential electronic systems installed in special buildings, rooms, areas, or environments, and where the value is high, require special treatment as described in MIL-HDBK-1008A and below:

4.4.2.1   Classification of Hazard. MIL-HDBK-1008A classifies all occupancies in accordance with the amount of combustibles and flammable liquids contained in the space and cites specific examples for each classification.

4.4.2.2   Fire Protection Systems. Systems appropriate for electronic facilities include wet-pipe sprinkler systems, dry-pipe pre-action sprinkler systems, carbon dioxide (CO_2) systems, halon systems and portable dry chemical extinguishers.

4.4.2.3   Fire Detection and Alarm Systems. See Section 5 for specific requirements.

4.4.2.4   HVAC System Interlocks. Specific requirements are given in NFPA 90A. Both MIL-HDBK-1008A and NFPA 90A indicate that, unless a specially designed smoke exhaust system is provided, HVAC equipment should be de-energized upon receipt of a fire or smoke alarm.

Section 5: ELECTRICAL ENGINEERING

5.1 <u>General</u>. All electronic facilities operated by the Navy, however varied in function, have similar requirements for electrical energy, grounding, bonding, and shielding, which are set forth below. In addition, all standard electrical criteria for naval shore facilities are applicable. Specific guidance for particular facilities will be contained in the BESEP. The designer must be concerned with the general requirements as well as the specifics in order to achieve an integrated and compatible electronic facility design.

5.2 <u>Electrical Power Requirements</u>. The ability of an electronic facility to perform its mission depends directly on the adequacy and reliability of the systems that supply and distribute its electrical power. An acceptable degree of power system reliability can be obtained only from the proper combination of primary, emergency, standby, uninterruptible, and conditioned power sources. Refer to MIL-HDBK-1004/1, <u>Electrical Engineering - Preliminary Design Considerations</u>, and MIL-HDBK-411, <u>Power and Environmental Control for Physical Plant OF DOD LONG HAUL COMMUNICATIONS</u>, Volume I and II.

5.2.1 <u>Power Sources</u>. The primary electrical power source should be supplied by a commercial power company. Two independent sources with two separate feeders are required where they are available and economically feasible (mission reliability/operational requirements versus cost). If commercial power sources are unavailable or inadequate, an on-station primary power plant is required. (Refer to MIL-HDBK-1004/1 for primary and alternate source selections and load estimation.) Technical equipment power requirements will be furnished by the project's electronic engineers (SPAWAR). Design electrical capacity shall be for 100 percent of station demand load. Spare capacity for a minimum of 25 percent of the total facility load shall be provided for future growth.

5.2.2 <u>Load Categories</u>. Electronic facility power loads are divided into categories (see Figure 6) according to function and allowable downtime.

5.2.2.1 <u>Station Load</u>. The station load is the total power requirement of the electronic facility.

5.2.2.2 <u>Nonoperational Load</u>. The nonoperational load refers to administrative, support, and miscellaneous power requirements not essential to facility operation and does not normally require emergency power.

5.2.2.3 <u>Operational Load</u>. The operational load is that portion of the load required to keep the facility in continuous operation. (The sum of the technical and nontechnical loads.)

5.2.2.4 <u>Nontechnical Load</u>. The nontechnical load is that part of the total operation load used for general lighting, convenience outlets, air conditioning, ventilating equipment, and other functions for normal operation and does not normally require emergency power.

5.2.2.5   <u>Technical Load</u>. The technical load is that portion of the operational load required for electronic equipment and ancillary equipment, including the lighting, air conditioning, and ventilation required for full continuity of facility function. The operation of the technical load is essential to the mission of the facility and normally requires emergency power.

5.2.2.6   <u>Noncritical Technical Load</u>. The noncritical load is that portion of the technical load not required for synchronous operation. This includes nonsynchronous electronic equipment, test equipment, emergency lighting, ventilation, and air conditioning for electronic equipment. The outage time tolerance for specific facilities will vary. Refer to BESEP for specific data.

5.2.2.7   <u>Critical Technical Load</u>. The critical technical load is that part of the total technical load required for continuous synchronous operation of electronic equipment. This includes any equipment that will malfunction during a momentary power dropout and cause additional outage after power is restored, as a result of the need to re-synchronize; loss of real time count by master time sources; or loss of data in ADP systems.

Government-furnished UPS equipment shall serve all critical technical loads. The BESEP will specify the loads to be served by the UFS as well as the size of the system.

5.2.3   <u>Electrical Power Characteristics</u>. Unless otherwise stated in the BESEP, the power characteristics normally will be as follows:

5.2.3.1   <u>Voltage</u>. Steady-state voltage variations shall not exceed plus or minus ten percent of the nominal voltage level.

a) For sites with separate power plants, the preferred voltage is 480Y/277.

b) For other power sources, the preferred voltage is 208Y/120 for loads less than or equal to 300 KVA and 480Y/277 for loads greater than 300 KVA.

5.2.3.2   <u>Frequency</u>. Steady-state frequency variations shall not exceed plus or minus five percent of the nominal frequency. The preferred frequency is 60 hertz (Hz). If 60 hz is not available overseas, 50 hz is normally supplied.

5.2.3.3   <u>Reliability</u>. For technical load bus, reliability shall be 99.99 percent, exclusive of scheduled outages, which must not exceed a total of 53 minutes during any 1 year.

5.2.3.4   <u>Dynamic or Transient Variation</u>. Limitations at the operational bus are:

a) Voltage; Minus 15 percent, plus 10 percent.

b) Frequency: Plus or minus 5 percent.

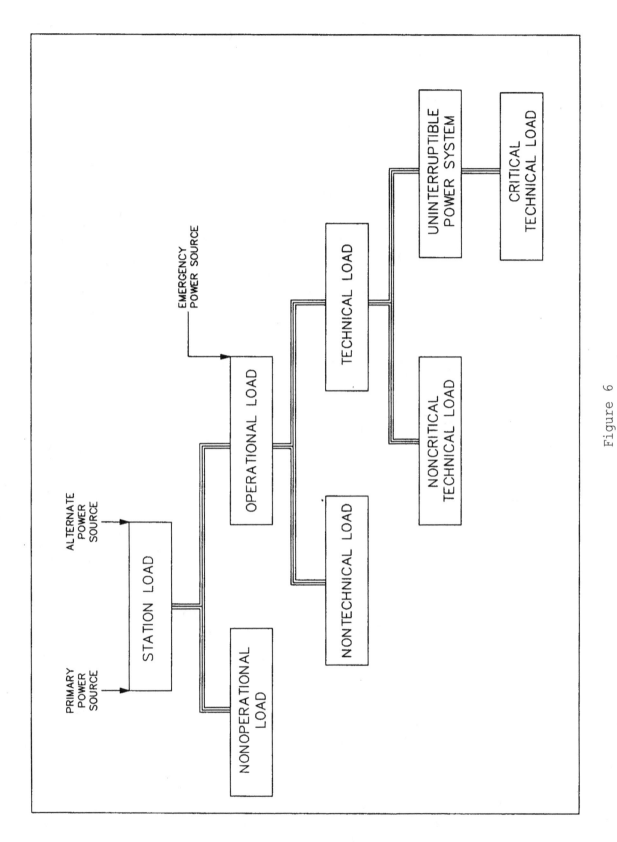

Figure 6
Power Load Categories

5.2.3.5   <u>Foreign Power</u>. Equipment and facilities to be operated in foreign countries shall be designed with the aforementioned power characteristics. If frequency conversion is required because of foreign power characteristics, a synchronous generator or solid state converter may be used. The input requirements and output capacity should be determined by the power available and the requirements of the equipment to be connected. Consideration should be given to standby requirements and location of the frequency conversion equipment. Generally, the frequency conversion equipment should be as close as feasible to the equipment being served.

5.2.4   <u>Emergency Power</u>. Emergency power systems (Class C, as defined in MIL-HDBK-411) enable restoration of power to the operational load within 10 to 60 seconds and provide power during short-term outages. These systems generally consist of a number of engine-driven generator sets and automatic transfer equipment. Emergency power system shall conform to MIL-HDBK-1004/1 and MIL-HDBK-411, and shall be designed to provide continuity of power during transfer from emergency source to primary source. Emergency power systems shall be capable of carrying 100 percent of the operational load as shown in Figure 6. The emergency power systems shall be rated at least 1.5 times the output rating of the UPS. For emergency power requirements in security areas, refer to Section 6 of this manual.

5.2.5   <u>Uninterruptible Power Sources (UPS)</u>. UPS (also referred to as no-break power or Class D auxiliary power) use stored energy to provide continuous power within specified voltages and frequency tolerances. UPS shall be provided for all critical technical loads. UPS systems will be government furnished. The installation shall be in accordance with MIL-HDBK-1004/1 and herein specified.

5.2.6   <u>Special Power Requirements</u>

5.2.6.1   <u>400-Hz Power</u>. Electronic facilities often require that power be supplied to equipment at a frequency of 400 hz. Two types of frequency conversion equipment are available: motor generators and static converters. The type and capacity of the units should be determined by the requirements of the equipment. Consideration should be given to standby requirements when selecting and locating frequency converters. Both types of converters must be adequately grounded to prevent electromagnetic interference. Power at 400 hz requires that the distribution system be carefully engineered. Consider the use of larger size conductors, parallel feeders, non-magnetic conduits and load drop compensators. All cables carrying 400-hz power shall be run in separate raceway systems. For further information, refer to NAVFAC DM-4.05, <u>400 HZ Generation and Distribution Systems.</u>

5.2.6.2   <u>Direct-Current Power Systems</u>. Electronic facilities often require several direct-current power supplies and distribution systems. The systems usually operate at 24 or 48 volts., These voltage supplies are normally furnished by SPAWAR, along with the electronic equipment they serve.

5.2.7   <u>Power Conditioning</u>. At electronic facilities, it is possible for classified information from processing devices to be inductively coupled into power lines; consequently, power distribution conductors entering areas where classified information is processed may need to be filtered at the area boundary. Specific guidance concerning the treatment of such power and signal cabling will be contained in the BESEP.

In general, primary power distribution and protection should be outside classified areas to facilitate access for maintenance. Normal power distribution design for electronic equipment areas requires consideration of the peculiarities of communication and electronic equipment. For example, low-level signals in the microvolt range and a large frequency spectral environment would suggest that power lines be routed as far away as possible from the nearest antenna. Radio-frequency noise sources such as generators, air conditioning compressors, and switchgear should be located to minimize physical and electrical interference with electronic equipment.

Voltage transient protection should be installed on both transient sources and power distribution points for electronic equipment. Commercial power conditioning equipment, containing instrumentation and alarm capabilities as well as active and passive protection devices, may be necessary to provide the quality of power appropriate to the equipment being supported.

5.2.8   Electrical Distribution Systems. The electrical distribution system shall be designed in accordance with NFPA 70 National Electrical Code. Consideration should be given to providing a flexible system that will meet the facility's future requirements. Electronic equipment is constantly being upgraded, modified, and replaced. Bus duct systems and cable trays may prove to be the most flexible system in areas where new equipment is expected or where frequent modification may occur. The BESEP will provide equipment lists with power requirements for each piece of electronic equipment, including maximum load, voltage characteristics, and special requirements. All main transformers serving electronic facilities shall have lightning protectors on both the primary and the secondary side of the transformer.

5.2.8.1   Load Category. Each load category shall be fed as shown in Figure 7.

5.2.8.2   Circuit Breakers. Separate circuit breakers shall be provided at power panels for each equipment rack, cabinet, or piece of electronic equipment. Individual pieces of equipment shall be connected to the panelboards by wiring run in cable racks or conduits or a combination of both. Bolt-on circuit breakers should be used in electronic facilities.

5.2.8.3   Cable Vaults. Most buildings require underground radio-frequency cable, communication cable (telephone type), control cable, and power cable. These cables shall enter the building through two cable vaults, one for signal cables and one for power cables, These vaults shall also house the protective devices used to prevent surges from entering the building. The vaults shall be designed in accordance with the latest safety standards.

5.2.8.4   Wiring. Wiring to each piece of equipment shall be sized to carry full load current. Maximum voltage drop shall be in accordance with NFPA 70.

5.2.8.5   <u>Receptacles</u>. All receptacles other than 120-volt, general-purpose convenience outlets shall be marked with voltage, amperage, phase, and frequency.

5.2.8.6   <u>Neutral Conductors</u>. Full-size neutral conductors shall be used throughout the distribution system. Requirements for oversized neutral conductors shall be provided in the BESEP.

5.2.8.7   <u>Grounding Conductors</u>. Greenwire equipment grounding conductors shall be sized in accordance with NFPA 70. Requirements for oversized grounding conductors shall be provided in the BESEP.

5.2.8.8   <u>Cableways</u>. Cable shall be routed through trays or ducts suspended overhead. When raised flooring is used, cable shall be run in conduit within the space under the floor in accordance with the requirements of NFPA 70.

5.2.8.9   <u>Bus Ducts</u>. Bus ducts may be used as required.

5.2.8.10   <u>Power Line Transient Protection</u>. Transient overvoltage disturbances varying in severity and rate of occurrence are found in all power distribution systems. Sensitive electronic equipment exposed to these transients may be disrupted or, in some cases, damaged. Therefore, surge protection using Metal Oxide Varistors (MOV's), or similar devices, shall be installed at the load side of the main distribution switchgear. Select an MOV with a rating of less than 125 percent of the root-mean-square (rms) line-to-ground voltage. It is recommended that the largest joule rating and the lowest clamping level for the specific rms voltage rating be selected.

5.3   <u>Lighting Systems</u>. Interior lighting, roadway lighting, protective lighting, and area lighting systems shall be designed in accordance with MIL-HDBK-1004/1. Lighting levels shall be in accordance with the latest revision of the Illuminating Engineers Society (IES) <u>Lighting Handbook</u>, and MIL-HDBK-1190. In case of conflict, MIL-HDBK-1190 takes precedence over IES criteria.

5.3.1   <u>Emergency Lighting</u>. Battery-powered emergency lighting units shall be provided in all operational spaces, including the emergency generator rooms and UPS rooms. All battery-powered emergency lighting units shall conform to the requirements of Federal Specification W-L-305, <u>Light Set, General Illumination (Emergency or Auxiliary)</u>. Special requirements shall be provided in the BESEP.

5.3.2   <u>Fluorescent Fixtures</u>. Unless otherwise specified in the BESEP, fluorescent fixtures may be used. Power line filters shall be installed as set forth in the BESEP.

5.3.3   <u>Consoles</u>. Consideration should be given to the use of indirect and/or dimmable lighting in equipment console operating spaces to reduce glare on equipment display panels.

5.3.4   <u>Antenna Areas</u>. Electric vapor lamps shall not be used within 1/2 mile (805 m) of receiving antennas.

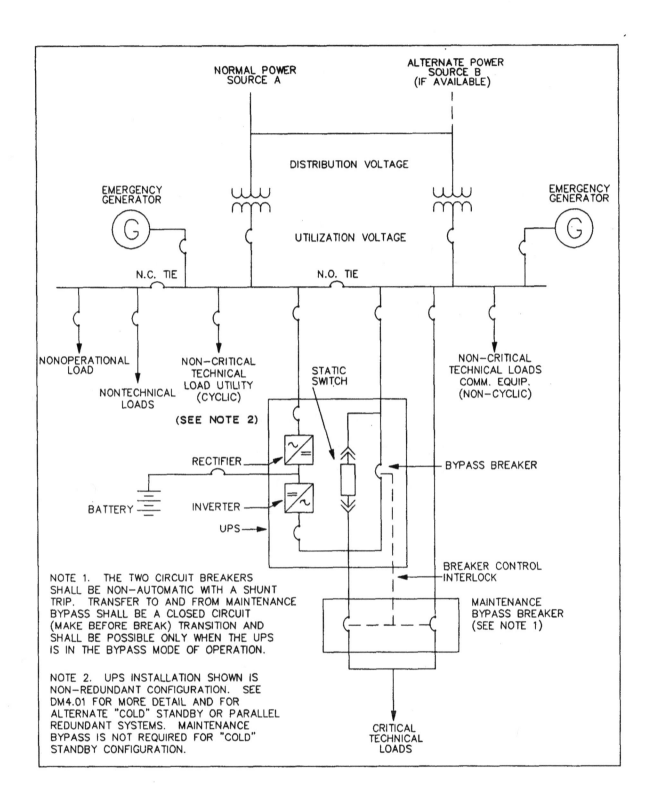

Figure 7
Typical Bus Configuration for New Facilities

5.3.5   Security Lighting. For security lighting criteria, refer to Section 6 of this manual.

5.4   Grounding. Bonding, and Shielding

5.4.1   Description. All grounding and bonding in new electronic facilities shall conform to MIL-STD-188/124, Grounding, Bonding and Shielding for Common Long Haul/Tactical Communication Systems, and MIL-HDBK-419. All shielding and (HEMP) protection shall satisfy the requirements set forth in the BESEP and MIL-HDBK-1012/2, High Altitude Electromagnetic Pulse Protection for Ground-Based Facilities. Requirements for specific facilities are set forth in Section 8 of this manual.

5.4.2   General Grounding Requirements

5.4.2.1   Facility Ground System Requirements. Recommended grounding practices for a typical electronic facility are illustrated in Figure 8. These recommended grounding practices can be modified when HEMP shielding is required and such modifications are provided in the BESEP.

       a)   Earth electrode subsystem (EES). The EES consists of a network of earth electrode rods, plates, mats, or grids and their interconnecting conductors.   For a detailed discussion, refer to MIL-HDBK-419, Chapter 2 of Volume I and Section 1.2 of Volume II.

       b) Lightning protection subsystem. This subsystem, consisting of air terminals, their down conductors, and related suppressors, provides a nondestructive path to ground for lightning energy contacting or induced in facility structures. For a detailed discussion, refer to MIL-HDBK-419, Chapter 3 of Volume I and Section 1.3 of Volume II.

       c)   Fault protection subsystem. This subsystem ensures that personnel are protected from shock and that equipment is protected from damage or destruction resulting from faults.   For a detailed discussion, refer to MIL-HDBK-419, Chapter 4 of Volume I and Section 1.4 of Volume I and Section 1.4 of Volume II.

       d) Signal reference subsystem. This subsystem established a voltage reference and minimizes noise currents in the facility, so that relative voltage levels are maintained and unacceptable noise voltages not occur on signal paths or circuits. For a detailed discussion, refer to MIL-HDBK-419, Chapter 5 of Volume I and Section 1.4 of Volume II.

5.4.2.2   Resistance   Requirements

       a)   Earth Electrode Subsystem. The basic measure of effectiveness of an earth electrode is the value in ohms of the resistance to earth at its input connection. MIL-STD-188/124A specifies 10 ohms as design goal to satisfy lightning protection requirements. NFPA 78, National Fire Protection Association's Lightning Protection Code, also recommend 10 ohms.

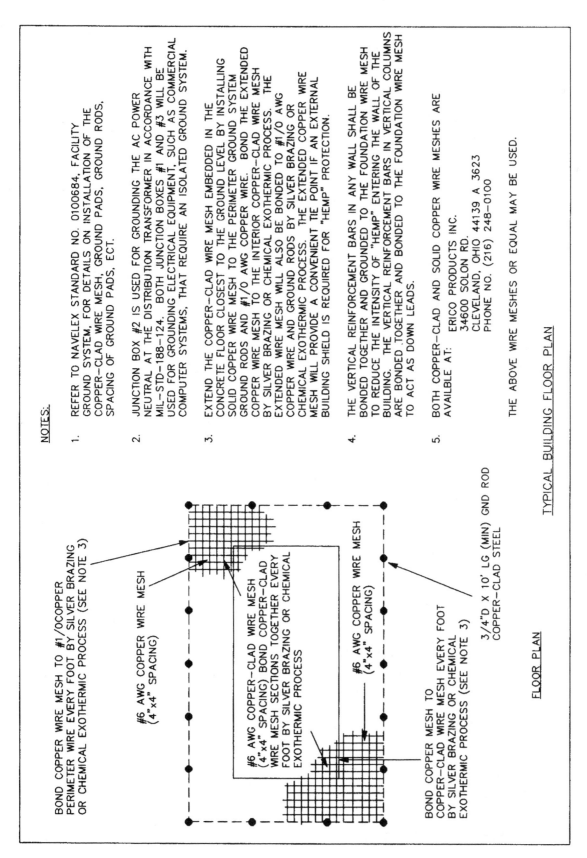

FLOOR PLAN

TYPICAL BUILDING FLOOR PLAN

Figure 8a
Typical Facility Ground System

NOTES:

1. REFER TO NAVELEX STANDARD NO. 0100684, FACILITY GROUND SYSTEM, FOR DETAILS ON INSTALLATION OF THE COPPER-CLAD WIRE MESH, GROUND PADS, GROUND RODS, SPACING OF GROUND PADS, ECT.

2. JUNCTION BOX #2 IS USED FOR GROUNDING THE AC POWER NEUTRAL AT THE DISTRIBUTION TRANSFORMER IN ACCORDANCE WITH MIL-STD-188-124. BOTH JUNCTION BOXES #1 AND #3 WILL BE USED FOR GROUNDING ELECTRICAL EQUIPMENT, SUCH AS COMMERCIAL COMPUTER SYSTEMS, THAT REQUIRE AN ISOLATED GROUND SYSTEM.

3. EXTEND THE COPPER-CLAD WIRE MESH EMBEDDED IN THE CONCRETE FLOOR CLOSEST TO THE GROUND LEVEL BY INSTALLING SOLID COPPER WIRE MESH TO THE PERIMETER GROUND SYSTEM GROUND RODS AND #1/0 AWG COPPER WIRE. BOND THE EXTENDED COPPER WIRE MESH TO THE INTERIOR COPPER-CLAD WIRE MESH BY SILVER BRAZING OR CHEMICAL EXOTHERMIC PROCESS. THE EXTENDED WIRE MESH WILL ALSO BE BONDED TO #1/0 AWG COPPER WIRE AND GROUND RODS BY SILVER BRAZING OR CHEMICAL EXOTHERMIC PROCESS. THE EXTENDED COPPER WIRE MESH WILL PROVIDE A CONVENIENT TIE POINT IF AN EXTERNAL BUILDING SHIELD IS REQUIRED FOR "HEMP" PROTECTION.

4. THE VERTICAL REINFORCEMENT BARS IN ANY WALL SHALL BE BONDED TOGETHER AND GROUNDED TO THE FOUNDATION WIRE MESH TO REDUCE THE INTENSITY OF "HEMP" ENTERING THE WALL OF THE BUILDING. THE VERTICAL REINFORCEMENT BARS IN VERTICAL COLUMNS ARE BONDED TOGETHER AND BONDED TO THE FOUNDATION WIRE MESH TO ACT AS DOWN LEADS.

5. BOTH COPPER-CLAD AND SOLID COPPER WIRE MESHES ARE AVAILBLE AT: ERICO PRODUCTS INC.
                            34600 SOLON RD.
                            CLEVELAND, OHIO 44139 A 3623
                            PHONE NO. (216) 248-0100

THE ABOVE WIRE MESHES OR EQUAL MAY BE USED.

BOND COPPER WIRE MESH TO #1/0COPPER PERIMETER WIRE EVERY FOOT BY SILVER BRAZING OR CHEMICAL EXOTHERMIC PROCESS (SEE NOTE 3)

#6 AWG COPPER WIRE MESH (4"x4" SPACING)

#6 AWG COPPER-CLAD WIRE MESH (4"x4" SPACING) BOND COPPER-CLAD WIRE MESH SECTIONS TOGETHER EVERY FOOT BY SILVER BRAZING OR CHEMICAL EXOTHERMIC PROCESS

#6 AWG COPPER WIRE MESH (4"x4" SPACING)

BOND COPPER MESH TO COPPER-CLAD WIRE MESH EVERY FOOT BY SILVER BRAZING OR CHEMICAL EXOTHERMIC PROCESS (SEE NOTE 3)

3/4"D X 10' LG (MIN) GND ROD COPPER-CLAD STEEL

39

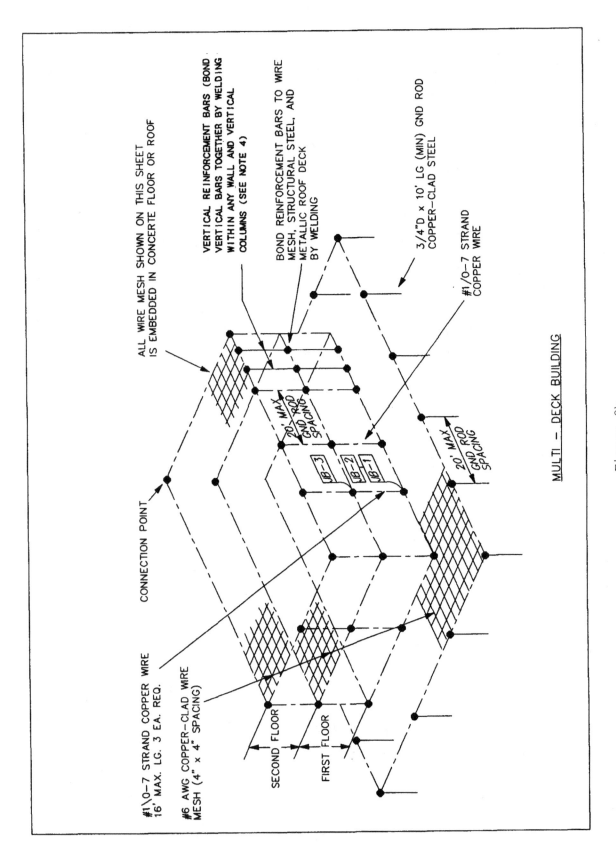

MULTI – DECK BUILDING

Figure 8b
Typical Facility Ground System

b) Fault protection subsystem. NFPA 70, in Article 250, requires that a single electrode consisting of a rod, pipe, or plate, and not having a resistance to ground of 25 ohms or less, be augmented by additional made electrodes.

c) Qualification of NFPA 70 resistance requirements. MIL-STD-188/124A establishes a design goal, of 10 ohms for facility ground systems. Where this is not possible, alternative methods should be considered for reducing resistance to the lowest feasible resistance-to-ground value. For detailed discussions and applications, refer to MIL-HDBK-419, Sections 2.6 and 2.9 of Volume I and Section 1.2 of Volume II.

d) Lightning protection subsystem. For lightning protection, a grounding resistance of 10 ohms or less is recommended. For a detailed discussion, refer to MIL-HDBK-419, Sections 2.6, 2.9, 3.7, and 3.8 of Volume I and Section 1.3 of Volume II.

5.4.3   <u>Specific Grounding Requirements</u>

5.4.3.1   <u>Electronic Equipment</u>. Each piece of electronic equipment shall be served by a green ground wire carried in the same cable or conduit as the power service to the equipment.

5.4.3.2   <u>Distribution Service</u>: The neutral of the distribution service. shall be grounded only at the main service entrance, at which point it shall be grounded to the EES.

5.4.3.3   <u>Security Fence</u>. Permanent security fencing normally requires a grounding system to ensure personnel safety and, in some instances, to prevent re-radiation of signals. Grounded security fence shall be constructed of galvanized chain-link fencing with bonded connections at all intersections, or with a No. 8 American Wire Gage (AWG) (minimum) copper conductor woven through the fabric of the entire length of the fence. The wire addition shall not be substituted for the top rail of the fence. The supporting posts and top rails shall be made of electrically conductive material. Both the fence posts and the fence fabric or conductor wire shall be grounded by an 8-foot ground rod at alternate fence posts. When a gate is incorporated, its hinges shall be bonded with flexible No. 8 AWG copper wire. These wires shall be connected to the gate post and the frame of the gate using exothermic welding or approved pressure connectors. No fencing material shall be installed which has been covered with non-conductive material.

5.4.4   <u>General Bonding Requirements</u>. Steel framing shall be bonded to the facility's ground system. Vertical columns shall be bonded at the top and bottom. Reinforcing steel shall be bonded 10 feet (3.05 m) on center each way, unless otherwise specified. Helix houses and most LF facilities have more stringent bonding requirements and shall be bonded according to the criteria set forth in this manual and the project BESEP.

5.4.5   <u>Specific Bonding Requirements</u>

5.4.5.1   <u>Cable Trays</u>. Cable trays shall be used as part of the overall system bonding scheme. Tray sections shall be bonded together to provide a continuous electrical path. Trays shall be bonded to equipment housings by wide, flexible, solid bond straps. For a detailed discussion, refer to MIL-HDBK-419, Section 1.7.4.1 of Volume II.

5.4.5.2 <u>Tubing and Conduit</u> Long spans of conduit shall be bonded to the structure at both ends and at several intermediate points.

a) Flexible conduit. A flared, split-sleeve clamp shall be used to prevent deformation of flexible conduit.

b) Rigid conduit. Ordinary clamps may be used on rigid conduit.

c) For a detailed discussion, refer to MIL-HDBK-419, Section 1.5.4.2 of Volume II.

5.4.6 <u>General Shielding Requirements</u>. Shielding requirements shall be as set forth in the BESEP. For a detailed discussion, refer to MIL-HDBK-419, Chapter 8 of Volume I, Section 1.6 of Volume II and MIL-HDBK-1012/2.

5.4.7 <u>Specific Shielding Requirements</u>

5.4.7.1 <u>Shielded Enclosures/Screen Rooms</u>. General requirements for attenuation are normally 60 dB for existing facilities and 100 dB for new facilities. Specific requirements shall be as set forth in the BESEP. Penetration holes and discontinuities are discussed in MIL-HDBK-419, Chapter 8 of Volume I and MIL-HDBK-1012/2.

5.4.7.2 <u>Tempest</u>. In general, shielding to provide security will require TEMPEST shielded enclosures. The normal attenuation is 100 dB. Specific requirements shall be as set forth in the BESEP.

5.4.7.3 HEMP HEMP protection shall be provided as indicated in MIL-HDBK-1012/2 and the BESEP.

5.5 <u>HEMP Protection</u>. The detonation of a nuclear device at high altitudes produces extremely high electromagnetic transients over a large geographical area. This phenomenon is referred to as HEMP. The primary effect of HEMP is the production of large voltages and currents in conductors such as power lines, telephone lines, metallic fences, buried cables, and antennas. These induced voltages and current may cause secondary effects, such as insulation flashover and equipment malfunction and/or damage. Solid-state electronic devices are especially susceptible to transients such as those produced by HEMP.

Consideration should be given to providing HEMP protection for all critical electronic facilities through the use of voltage-limiting surge arresters, low-pass filters, shielding, and other devices such as varistors and carbon blocks. Bonding and grounding requirements for HEMP protection are set forth in MIL-HDBK-1012/2. Shielding requirements for HEMP protection will be specified in MIL-HDBK-1012/2 and the BESEP.

5.6 <u>Energy Conservation</u>. Every effort should be made during design to minimize the use of energy over the life of a facility, insofar as the facility's mission and system reliability will allow. Where energy monitoring and control systems (EMCS) are already installed on the base, consider adding the new facility to the system. Refer to NAVFAC DM-4.09, _Energy Monitoring and Control Systems_, for design methods in accordance with NFGS 13947, _EMCS, Large System Configuration_, through 13950, _EMCS, Micro System Configuration_. In addition, the following items should be considered:

5.6.1   _Metering_. Provide metering to measure energy consumption. Consider kilowatt-hour and demand meters for the total facility, operational load bus, and technical load bus.

5.6.2   _Power Factor_. Maintain a high power factor; provide power factor correction, when required, to maintain a minimum power factor of 85 percent at peak load.

5.6.3   _Motors_. All motors 1 horsepower and above shall be three-phase motors. Consider high-efficiency motors for all HVAC and auxiliary equipment.

5.6.4   _Lighting_. General illumination levels should not exceed specified levels. Provide task lighting to supplement general lighting, as required.

5.6.5   _Lighting Control_. Provide additional switching to reduce energy used for lighting unoccupied areas.

5.7   _Fire Alarm and Detection Systems_. Fire alarm and detection systems shall provide maximum fire protection for personnel and equipment consistent with the function of the facility. Fire alarm and detection systems shall conform to the requirements of MIL-HDBK-1008, NFPA 72A, _Standard for the Installation. Maintenance. and Use of Local Protective Signaling Systems for Guard's Tour, Fire Alarm. and Supervisory Service_, and NFPA 72E, _Automatic Fire Detectors_. Electronic facilities shall be provided with manual and automatic fire reporting systems to transmit the following signals:

5.7.1   _Onsite Signal_. To building occupants, to permit prompt corrective action and/or evacuation.

5.7.2   _Offsite Signal_. To fire department headquarters or another central office that will implement emergency action.

5.7.3   _System Signal_. To actuate automatic fire extinguishing equipment.

Because overheating or malfunctioning electronic equipment must be detected as early as possible, automatic supervision of all alarm circuits shall be provided. Automatic fire detection shall be provided in electronic equipment areas, in record storage rooms, and under raised floors.

5.8   _Signal Systems_. Design of signal systems shall be as specified in NAVFAC DM-4.07, _Wire Communication and Signal Systems_.

THIS PAGE INTENTIONALLY LEFT BLANK

Section 6: PHYSICAL SECURITY

6.1   General. Physical security is concerned with limiting, controlling, or preventing personnel access to specific areas. A sound physical security program is the result of good planning. The best and most economical programs are those incorporated in the facility's design and construction. The facility's configuration and location; the use of barriers, protective lighting, particular kinds of construction, intrusion detection alarms, closed circuit television (CCTV), and security fencing; and the guard communication network must be coordinated with the using agency to ensure conformance with the installation's security plan. The mode of operation, level of security, and designer's responsibility for particular security elements will be designated in the BESEP.

6.2   Exterior Physical Security. External security requirements in most cases depend on the internal security measures provided in the facility design and on the type of protection required. Normally, external considerations, including building location and orientation and the use of protective barriers and lighting, are developed as part of the facility's security plan and specified in the BESEP. DIAM 50-3, Physical Security Standards for Sensitive Compartmented Information Facilities, and MIL-HDBK-1013/1 should be the primary criteria sources for design of the required facilities.

6.2.1   Perimeter Fencing. Generally, chain-link fencing is used for permanent areas. General-purpose barbed tape obstacle and concertina wire are used for temporary installations or where the terrain does not allow construction of chain-link fencing. Dual perimeter barriers are described in DIAM 50-3. Alternative fence configurations are discussed in MIL-HDBK-1013/1. The following requirements are the minimum for normal protection:

        a) Unless otherwise specified, the perimeter security fence shall be at least 50 feet (15.24 m) from enclosed structures (except guard shelters). A clear zone not less than 20 feet (6.1 m) wide shall be provided immediately outside the fence. This area shall be devoid of buildings, parking areas, poles, guy line anchors, shrubs, trees, sign boards, and any other object that could conceal personnel. Grass is permissible, provided it is kept mowed. A similar clear zone at least 50 feet (15.24 m) wide shall be provided immediately inside the fence. This area shall meet the requirements of the exterior clear zone, except that approved guard shelters and protective lighting poles may be installed.

        b) Chain-link fencing shall conform to the latest issue of Federal Specification RR-F-191, Fencing, Wire (Chain-Link Fabric). The fence fabric shall be 6 feet (1.83 m) high, unless other requirements are provided by the sponsor. The fence shall be topped by a 45-degree outrigger that is 15 to 18 inches (381 to 457.2 mm) long. Three evenly spaced strands of barbed wire shall be attached to the outriggers. All fence fabric and barbed wire strands shall be grounded.

        c) Utility openings, covers, sewers, culverts, tunnels, and other subsurface routes which penetrate the fence line shall be protected in accordance with DIAM 50-3.

d) The number of gates and perimeter entrances shall be reduced to the minimum required for safe and efficient operation.

e) Guard shelters shall be provided when required by the BESEP.

6.2.2   Security Lighting. Lighting shall be installed inside the perimeter security fence in a manner to illuminate the fence completely and to prevent an intruder from using the light poles and guy wires to gain access to the area. Illumination shall be in accordance with the lighting specifications in Tables 20 and 21 of MIL-HDBK-1013/1.

a) Illuminate areas shadowed by structures.

b) Ensure that failure of one lamp in a circuit will not affect other lamps in the same circuit.

c) Provide overlapping light distribution to minimize reductions in illumination levels upon lamp failure.

d) Protect all components of the system from vandalism.

e) Provide lights on buildings.

f) Provide an emergency power generator within the security area.

The emergency power source shall be adequate to sustain protective lighting of all critical areas and structures for 8 hours and shall go into operation automatically when the primary power fails. The facility shall have generator- or battery-powered lights at key control points in case a failure disables the secondary power supply.

g) Install special-purpose lighting (such as for fog penetration) when climatic or other local factors dictate.

h) Provide additional lighting for (CCTV) security surveillance, as necessary.

6.2.3   Protective Alarm Systems. Operational sites constructed in accordance with physical security criteria set forth in this manual normally will not require extensive protective alarm systems. The Equipment Application Guide for Joint-Service Interior Intrusion Detection System (J-SIIDS) Equipment provides information on intrusion detection alarm devices that meet most Navy requirements. The BESEP or the user command will provide specific intrusion detection system requirements.

6.2.4   CCTV. Because of reduced personnel levels, CCTV may be required to supplement the guard force. The BESEP or the user command will specify these requirements, if applicable.

6.3   Interior Physical Security

6.3.1   Delay Times. Guidelines for selecting and designing facility components to meet specified delay times are provided in MIL-HDBK-1013/1

Procedures for determining delay times, if not specified by the BESEP or the user command, are given in MIL-HDBK-1013/1.

6.3.2   Building Layout. Portions of the building requiring special security consideration will be identified by the BESEP or by the user command.

6.3.3   Wall Construction. Secure area wall construction shall be 4 inches (100 mm) of reinforced concrete or 8 inches (200 mm) of solid masonry, normally without windows and with controlled access. For detailed requirements, refer to DIAM 50-3.

6.3.4   Roof and Floor Construction. At least 4 inches (100 mm) of reinforced concrete will normally be used for roof and floor construction. Hardening methods for other types of construction are provided in MIL-HDBK-1013/1. False ceilings or raised floors may provide a means of concealment. These ceilings or floors are considered part of the protected area to which they are attached, and the true walls, floor, and ceiling must meet the applicable requirements. Suspended false ceilings shall have at least one "quick-remove" access panel 18 by 18 inches (460 by 460 mm) for each 400 square feet (ft^2) (37.2 square meters (m^2)) of ceiling area. Raised floors must be similarly equipped.

6.3.5   Perimeter Doors. Entry and exit doors of secure areas shall be as specified in the BESEP or DIAM 50-3. Normally, a 1-3/4-inch (44.5 mm) solid wood door will suffice for a continuously operating facility.

6.3.6   Windows. Windows are not authorized in secure areas.

6.3.7   Air Vents and Ducts Vents, ducts and other openings that breach the facility perimeter require protection as specified in DIAM 50-3. Normally, any opening which exceeds 6 inches (152.4 mm) requires protection.

6.3.8   Miscellaneous Hardware

6.3.8.1   Roof Doors and Hatches. Roof doors and hatches shall be internally secured with padlocks and hasps in conformance with the provisions of Military Specification (Mil Spec.) MIL-P-43607, Padlock, Key Operated, High Security, Shrouded Shackle. Roof doors may also be equipped with a cylindrical case or bored lockset. Such locksets, when installed, shall be mounted with the lock cylinder to the exterior.

6.3.8.2   Coded Locks. If required for control of routine access, an electrically controlled and operated latch mechanism for interior doors shall be installed. RF emissions shall meet the requirements of MIL-STD-461, Electromagnetic Emission and Susceptibility Requirements for the Control of Electromagnetic Interference, for class II-A equipment. Such mechanisms shall not mate or interface with other required locksets. Separate surface-mounted night latches or specialty hardware shall be added to the door to accommodate the electrically operated mechanism. Key-operated bypass cylinders are not authorized.

6.3.9   <u>Vaults</u>. Vaults or vault construction will be specified by the BESEP or the user command. Specific criteria for construction and installation are given in DIAM 50-3.

6.3.9.1   <u>Safety and Emergency Devices</u>. Vault doors shall be equipped with an emergency escape device and with the following:

   a) A luminous light switch.

   b) An emergency light (if the vault is otherwise unlighted).

   c) An interior alarm switch or other device (such as a telephone) to permit a person in the vault to communicate with a vault custodian, guard, or guard post.

   d) Instructions on obtaining release shall be permanent affixed to the inside of the door or prominently displayed elsewhere inside the vault.

   e) A bank vault ventilator approved by Underwriters Laboratories, Inc., if the vault is not otherwise served by forced air ventilation.

6.3.9.2   <u>Fire Protection</u>. The vault shall be equipped with at least one CO_2 fire extinguisher approved by Underwriters Laboratories (UL), Inc.

Section 7: SAFETY

7.1   General. The presence of Electromagnetic Radiation (EMR) at transmitter sites poses potential hazards to personnel, including direct exposure to EMR, shock and burns, and detonation of fuel and ordnance. The presence of transmitting and receiving structures at communication sites poses potential hazards to aircraft. SPAWAR normally will identify and analyze these hazards during site selection, and will be responsible for planning site layout to eliminate or avoid them. The project BESEP will identify any protective measures required. The designer must be aware of the hazards associated with these facilities, and, during the normal phases of design, shall bring them to the attention of the agency responsible for the design. Other hazards associated with electronic facilities include electrical shock, electrical fire, toxic and explosive gases from batteries, ozone from corona discharge and noise from teletypes and cooling fans. Facilities must include adequate electrical isolation, insulation, fire protection, ventilation, and acoustical absorption to provide a safe and healthful environment.

7.2   Human Engineering. The designer must consider safety not only in relation to operator functions and accessibility for maintenance and repair, but also in relation to physical layout for traffic, interface with other equipment, and environmental factors, such as lighting, temperature, and humidity. The basic references are MIL-STD-882, System Safety Program Requirements, and MIL-STD-1472, Human Engineering Design Criteria for Military Systems, Equipment and Facilities.

7.3   Radiation Hazards

7.3.1   Hazards to Personnel. RF radiation can be harmful if the body absorbs radiated energy and physical contact with induced voltages can result in shock or RF burns.

7.3.1.1   Absorbed Radiation

a) Personnel exposure limits to RF radiation are defined in OPNAVNOTE 5100, Ser 45/5U394867 of 30 July 1985, Personnel Protection Policy for Exposure to Radio-Frequency Radiation (RFR). Personnel shall not be exposed to a power density which, when averaged over any 0.1-hour period, exceeds those values listed in Table 3 in the frequency domain of 10 kHz - 300 GHz. Neither the root mean squared electric field strength (E) nor the root mean squared magnetic field strength (H) may exceed those values when averaged over any 0.1-hour period (refer to Table 3).

Table 3
Equivalent Permissible Exposure Limits For Unrestricted Areas

FREQUENCY (MHz)	POWER DENSITY (mW/cm²)	ELECTRIC FIELD STRENGTH SQUARED (V²/m²)	MAGNETIC FIELD STRENGTH SQUARED (A²/m²)
0.01-3	100	400,000	2.5
3-30	$900/f^2$	$4000(900/f^2)$	$0.025(900/f^2)$
30-300	1.0	4000	0.025
300-1500	$f/300$	$4000(f/300)$	$0.025(f/300)$
1500-300,000	5.0	20,000	0.125

NOTES: 1)   When both the electric field and magnetic field are measured, use the more restrictive value.
2)   Tables apply only to whole body exposures and are based on the overall PEL.
3)   f is the frequency in Megahertz (MHz).

Where exposure is intermittent or the exposure level varies over 0.1-hour period, the equivalent energy fluence level of 1 mW-hr/cm² may be used as the limit of exposure for any 0.1-hour period. All areas in which RF levels exceed prescribed limits are considered hazardous and shall be identified with currently adopted RF hazard warning signs.

b)   The area in the vicinity of HF transmitting antennas is hazardous and shall be restricted to prevent inadvertent entry. In all cases, entry into hazardous areas shall be controlled to prevent exposure of personnel to power levels in excess of the prescribed limits.

c)   The minimum safe distance from specific transmitting antennas and the maximum exposure time within these distances under certain modes of operation are listed in NAVSEA OP3565/NAVAIR 16-1-529/NAVELEX 0967-LP-6240-6010, Volume I, Technical Manual Electromagnetic Radiation Hazards (U).

7.3.1.2   Shock and RF Burn Hazards. EMR from transmitting antennas can induce voltages in metallic objects, resulting in shocks or burns to personnel. The induced voltages may produce open sparks or arcs when contact between conductive objects is made or broken. Hazards caused by RF-induced voltages can be reduced considerably by proper grounding and bonding of buildings and equipment, as discussed in Section 5 of this handbook. Wherever such equipment exists, the hazardous area shall be enclosed with a fence.

7.3.2   Hazards of Electromagnetic Radiation to Ordnance (HERO). Electromagnetic radiation, under certain conditions, can detonate Electro-Explosive Devices (EED's) contained in ordnance materials. NAVSEA OP3565/NAVAIR 16-1-529/NAVELEX 0967-LP-624-6010, Volume II, Part One, lists three classifications of ordnance materials based on their susceptability to radiation hazard: (1) HERO SAFE, (2) HERO SUSCEPTIBLE, and (3) HERO UNSAFE.

7.3.2.1   <u>Hero Unsafe</u>. HERO UNSAFE ordnance materials are the most susceptible to RF radiation and constitute the "worst-case" situation for shore communication transmitters. An ordnance item is defined as HERO UNSAFE when any of the following conditions exist:

(a) When its internal wiring is physically exposed.

(b) When additional electrical connections are required for the item being tested.

(c) When EED's with exposed wire leads are handled or loaded.

(d) When the item is being assembled or disassembled.

(e) When the item remains disassembled.

7.3.2.2   <u>Exemption</u>. Ordinance items may be exempted from the HERO UNSAFE classification as the result of previous HERO tests or analyses which are recorded for specific equipment in the NAVSEA/NAVAIR directive.

7.3.2.3   <u>Field Intensity Measurements</u>. Measurements of field intensity will ascertain the magnitude of an electromagnetic field. The field intensity of electromagnetic fields at communication frequencies (100 kHz to 1000 MHz) is referred to in terms of vertical electric field strength in units of volts per meter. A chart in NAVSEA OP3565/NAVAIR 16-1-529/NAVELEX 0967-LP-624-6010 indicates that, for HERO UNSAFE ordnance, the maximum safe field intensity is 0.2 V/m throughout the 2 to 32 MHz frequency range. This criterion could become a stringent restriction for radiation from communication transmitters of reasonably high power.

7.3.2.4   <u>Hero Safe.</u> HERO SAFE ordnance systems are not susceptible to radiation under any condition.

7.3.2.5   <u>Hero Susceptible</u>. Many ordnance systems are classified as HERO SUSCEPTIBLE under most conditions. The maximum safe field intensity prescribed for HERO SUSCEPTIBLE ordnance is 2.0 V/m from approximately 3.7 to 10.1 MHz frequency range.

7.3.2.6   <u>Safe Distances</u>. Since the maximum safe field intensity varies widely for the three classifications of ordnance, it is important to ascertain whether ordnance systems will be handled or stored in the vicinity of a transmitter site. Refer to NAVSEA OP3565/NAVAIR-16-1-529/ NAVELEX 0967-LP-624-6010 for safe distances from specific antennas.

If so, the classification of the ordnance most sensitive to RF radiation will determine the maximum field strength that can be tolerated.

7.3.3   <u>Fuel Hazards</u>. General guidance to prevent hazards to fueling in an RF environment are provided in NAVSEA OP3565/NAVAIR 16-1-529/NAVELEX 0967-LP-624-6010 Volume 1 and is as follows: Transmitters with 250 watts radiated output or less should not be installed within 50 feet (15 m) of fuel-handling or fueling areas. Transmitters with over 250 watts radiated output should not be installed within 200 feet (61 m) of fuel-handling or fueling areas. In no case should power density in the fueling area be greater than would exist at a distance of 50 feet (15 m) from radiated output of 250 watts. See Figure 9.

7.3.3.1   <u>Bonding and Grounding</u>. Where space limitations require the location of fueling stations, parking ramps, or other structures near an antenna site, all metal used in wooden structures within 200 feet (61 m) of fixed antennas radiating 250 watts or more shall be bonded together and grounded to reduce interference and fire hazards.

7.3.3.2   <u>Antenna Position</u>. If possible, antennas shall be positioned to prevent radiation of fueling areas while in operation. Otherwise, minimum distances given above shall be employed.

7.4   <u>Isolation and Warning Devices</u>

7.4.1   <u>Fence</u>. Only nonconducting materials are suitable for protective fences for antennas. Usually, a wood fence from 4 to 6 feet high (1.2 to 1.8 m) will provide adequate protection. Gates shall be designed and installed so that accidental entry into the hazardous area is not possible.

7.4.2   <u>Warning Signs</u>. Carefully worded and illustrated signs shall be posted conspicuously to prevent personnel from contacting high-voltage leads such as antennas and power supplies. Signs shall warn of the danger from all forms of radiation and from all other sources. Warning signs for RF-radiation hazards should be placed at eye level at the foot of ladders or other means of access to all towers, masts, or structures where hazardous levels of radiation occur or are likely to occur. In foreign countries, warning signs shall be posted in English and in the appropriate foreign language, using warning symbols appropriate for the country. Appropriate "HIGH-VOLTAGE" warning signs shall be permanently and conspicuously posted in hazardous areas.

7.4.3   <u>Equipment Shielding</u>. To avoid EMI and RADHAZ problems, the designer should take advantage of all inherent shielding offered by the installation or system, as well as the terrain. Building components, partitions, towers, and other similar structures may be used to advantage. Equipment in a console or rack may be placed to take advantage of the inherent shielding of the rack. Refer to NAVELEX 0101,106.

7.5   <u>Obstruction Lighting and Marking</u>. Poles and towers which are a hazard to aircraft must be suitably marked for daytime visibility and lighted at night by obstruction lights. A typical lighting system consists of a double light fixture, a transfer relay, and a photoelectric control unit which automatically turns the lights on at dusk and off at dawn. The markings and the number of lights required for a tower depend on its height. Refer to NAVELEX 0101,104. Tower lighting and marking shall comply with the latest revision of Federal Aviation Agency (FAA) AC 70/7460, <u>Obstruction Marking and Lighting</u>.

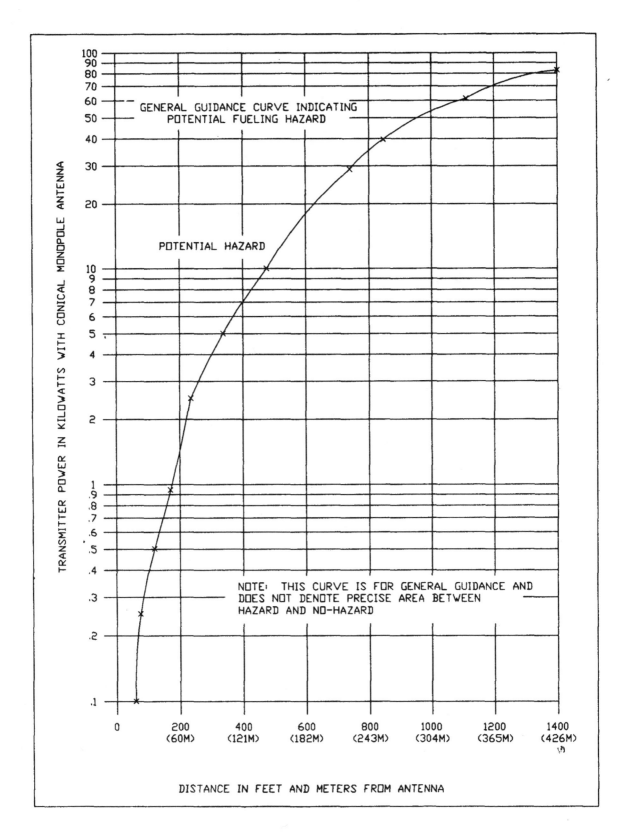

Figure 9
General Guidance Curve Indicating Potential Fueling Hazards

7.6   _Hazards Analysis_. When required, the designer may be responsible for preparing an analysis to define areas that may be hazardous to personnel and material, on the basis of presently accepted safe radiation limits. This analysis may be performed by combining theoretical "worst-case" calculations and onsite measurements of EMR power densities. For the purposes of analysis, the major source of hazardous electromagnetic energy is considered to be the antennas associated with radar and communication equipment of both low- and high- power emissions. The analysis shall be in accordance with NAVELEX 0101,106, _Electromagnetic Compatibility and Electromagnetic Radiation Hazards_. Other hazards analyses, where appropriate, must be conducted for other sources of radiation (laser, x-rays), and for compliance with the OSHA standards, 29CFR1910 and standards set forth in OPNAVINST 5100.23B, _Navy Occupational Safety and Health Program Manual_, and NAVELEX 0101.110A. All personnel work stations shall be ergonomically designed.

7.6.1   _Laser Safety_. Laser Safety criteria are defined in NAVELEXINST 5100.12, _Navy Laser Hazards Prevention Program_ and NAVMEDCOMINST 6470.2, _Laser Radiation Health Hazards_. All laser facilities shall incorporate the requirements of MIL-STD-1425. Laser installations and fiber optics installations shall be so designed that personnel (including maintenance personnel) will never view radiation levels in excess of those specified by NAVMEDCOMINST 6470.2.

7.6.2   _Ionizing Radiation Safety_. Ionizing radiation safety criteria such as that for X-rays are defined in NAVMED P-5055, _Radiation Health Protection Manual_ and NAVSEA OP3565/NAVAIR 16-1-529/NAVELEX 0967-LP-624-6010.

Section 8: COMMUNICATION/ELECTRONIC (C/E) FACILITIES

8.1   General. Because of differing functions, each facility within an electronic complex has certain specific design criteria. Specific guidance tailored to these and more general requirements will be contained in the BESEP. The designer must be concerned with both the general and specific requirements to achieve an integrated electronic facility design. The criteria set forth herein apply to the following types of facilities:

> Communication Centers
> Transmitter Buildings
> Receiver Buildings
> Direction-Finder Facilities
> Command/Control/Intelligence Centers
> Training Facilities
> Naval Air Station Control Towers
> Satellite Communication Ground Stations
> Transportables
> Automatic Data Processing Centers
> Oceanographic Facilities

8.2   Communication Centers. A communication center, normally in combination with a transmitter station and a receiver station, makes up a Naval communication station. The mission of a communication center is to receive, transmit, and deliver messages. It is the control, routing, and processing portion of the communication complex. The building contains areas required for the introduction, processing, and receipt of communication traffic to and from the communication systems. The center has access to the terminal ends of many communication links. It is provided with telephone trunk lines and may contain a telephone exchange facility. For further information, refer to NAVELEX 0101,102. For typical building layout, refer to Figure 10.

8.2.1   Architectural and Structural. In addition to the requirements in Section 3, all computer installations in communication centers require raised flooring.

8.2.2   Mechanical. For general requirements, refer to Section 4, Mechanical Engineering. Compressed air and water are normally required. Consult the BESEP for specific guidance.

8.2.3   Electrical

8.2.3.1 Lighting. Lighting shall be fluorescent.

8.2.3.2 Cables. Transmission lines may be brought into the building either above or below ground.

8.2.3.3 Cable Vaults. Cable vaults are normally included in communication center buildings.

8.2.3.4   Cable Trays. Provisions shall be made for installation of cable trays as required by the BESEP.

8.2.3.5   Emergency Power. An emergency power source shall be provided as set forth in the BESEP.

a) No-break power. Class D no-break shall be provided as designated in the BESEP.

b) All communication equipment not connected to no-break power shall be fed from the technical load bus.

8.2.3.6   Grounding. Red/black grounding in accordance with MIL-HDBK-419 is normally required in communication centers.

8.2.3.7   Shielding. When required, shielded rooms and attenuation requirements shall be as set forth in the BESEP.

8.3   Transmitter Buildings. A transmitter station consists of transmitting antennas and one or more buildings to house electronic equipment. The transmitter station is provided with communication links using microwave radio and land lines between the facility, the communication center, the receiver site, and the control tower, as required. Helix houses associated with low-frequency systems are discussed in Section 9 of this manual. For further information, refer to NAVELEX 0101,102. For one type of building layout, refer to Figure 11.

8.3.1   Architectural and Structural. In addition to the general requirements of Section 3, ventilated transmitter buildings normally are cruciform in shape, allowing for two rows of transmitters in the wings. A truck-loading platform shall be provided at the end of each transmitter wing to permit access for the largest equipment or equipment subsection. The control area shall be centrally located between the wings and the administrative, shop, and maintenance areas in adjacent space. Details will be set forth in the BESEP.

8.3.2   Mechanical. Transmitters liberate significant quantities of waste heat making air conditioning impracticable except where very small or very few transmitters are involved. The waste heat from large transmitter facilities should be removed either by ventilation or by heat exchange methods. The features of each are specified in paras. 8.3.2.1 and 8.3.2.2.

8.3.2.1   Ventilation. Requires the system to be arranged so that tempered ventilating air can enter the intake on the rear of the transmitter and so that the hot exhaust air at the top of the transmitter can be removed without the use of ducting that would, or could, exceed the static pressure capability of the fans within the transmitter and without short circuiting hot air into the transmitter intake or into the operators space.

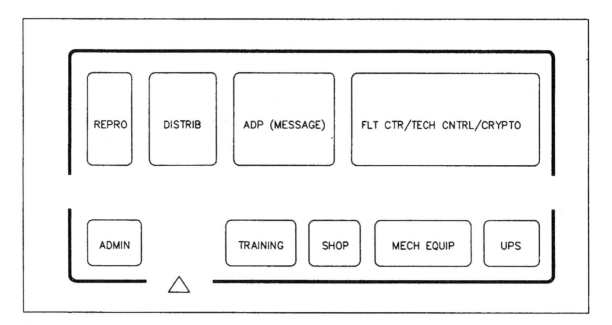

Figure 10
Functional Layout Typical Communication Center

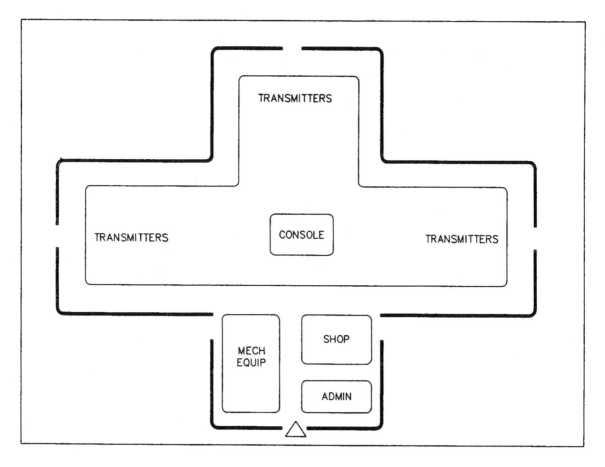

Figure 11
Functional Layout Typical Transmitter Building

This is usually accomplished through use of a "corridor/plenum" concept where the transmitters are placed in parallel rows facing each other within a long wing like structure. Partitions between the transmitters and a false ceiling above separate the operators workspace (corridor) that is air conditioned from the ventilated plenum behind the transmitters.

For proper operation this system requires :

a) That the incoming outside air to the plenum be tempered (warmed) by some of the waste heat being exhausted so as to stay above the highest dewpoint of the outside air to prevent condensation on the inside of the front face of the transmitter. Ninety degrees F (32 degrees C) is 5 degrees F above the highest dewpoint worldwide as listed in MIL-STD-210.

b) That the conditioned corridor temperature also be maintained at a value no less than 5 degrees F below the outside air dewpoint to prevent condensation on the inside of the front face of the transmitter. Eighty degrees F (27 degrees C) and 50 ± 10 percent relative humidity meets this requirement and shall be used.

c) That the incoming ventilating air be properly filtered.

d) That a draft hood be placed over the transmitter to collect the hot exhaust air so that spillover into the room will not occur. This allows a lower supply air temperature to be maintained (untempered outside air temperature plus 5 degrees F only) and less air to be moved (smaller or fewer fans).

e) That a proper control system he utilized to vary the tempering air to suit a wide range of ambient conditions. Such a system is described in Figure 4-4 of NAVELEX 0101,102. This will include thermostats, dampers, damper motors, hoods, filters etc.

8.3.2.2 <u>Heat Exchange</u>. Heat exchange is a system of extracting the heat at the transmitter exhaust port by latent change of a refrigerant in an evaporator and transporting the heat via the refrigerant gas to outside condensers where the heat is released and from where the liquid refrigerant runs back to the evaporator. This system was developed by NAVFACENGCOM Chesapeake Division (CHESDIV) and is described in U.S. Patent Office as statutory invention registration number H8 dated 7 Jan 86 (see Figure 12). Performance of the system is dependent upon the differential between the transmitter exhaust temperature (200 degrees F or more) and the outside ambient temperature (100 degrees F or less). In most locations at least 80 percent of the waste heat will be removed so that it is reasonable to remove the remaining heat by air conditioning which will also provide humidity control. Salient features of this (the recommended) system are:

a) A completely conditioned environment for both the equipment and the operators is provided.

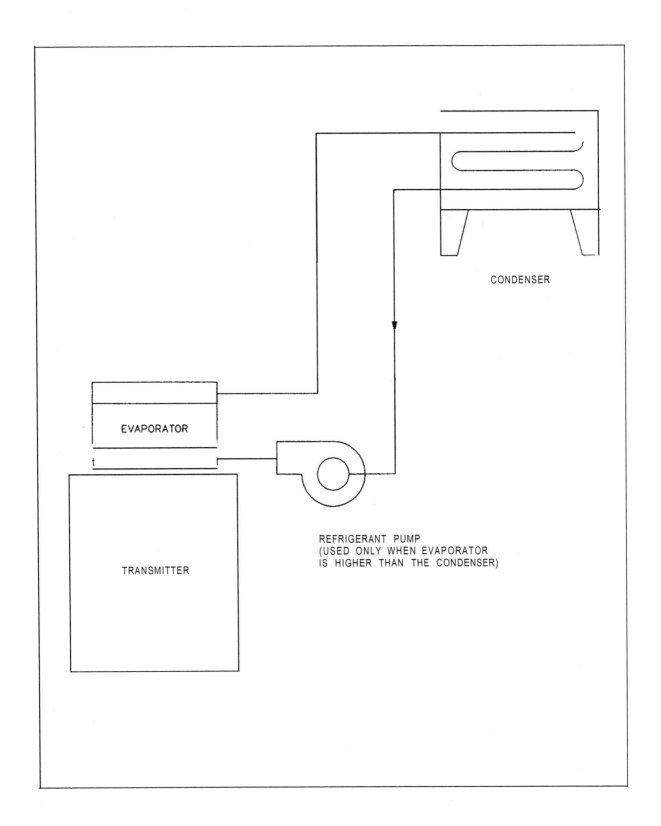

Figure 12
Heat Exchange System

b) This system does <u>not require</u>:

    (1) A building with long wings (cruciform shape) to permit ventilation.

    (2) Plenum/corridor partitions and false ceilings.

    (3) Walking the length of the corridor through a door and back to obtain access to the rear of the transmitter if adequate transmitter spacing is used.

    (4) A large number of outside air filters that must be either replaced periodically at high cost or cleaned which is labor intensive.

    (5) A large number of or large size fan for air circulation.

    (6) A complicated control system of ducts, dampers diffusers, control motors and sensors.

    c) The system <u>will provide controlled heating</u> of the space by simple thermostatic control of its heat removal capability.

    d) Failure of the heat exchange capability (such as loss of refrigerant) will not prevent the transmitter from operating.

    e) Loss of refrigerant is not hazardous in that it is non-toxic, non-flammable, has a saturated temperature above freezing at atmospheric pressure (will not freeze flesh) and is not a severe solvent. Therefore, loss would not pose a threat to either equipment or personnel.

    This system, as noted above, is the recommended method to environmentally control transmitter facilities, either large or small.

8.3.3   <u>Electrical</u>

8.3.3.1   <u>Lighting</u>. Fluorescent lighting may be used in all transmitter buildings except helix houses.

8.3.3.2   <u>Cable Vaults</u>. Cables shall enter the building through a cable vault, either under or above ground.

8.3.3.3   <u>Cabling</u>. Power cables shall be routed through cable trenches. Signal cables shall be run overhead, using cable hangers.

8.3.3.4   <u>Shielding</u>. When specified in the BESEP, the electronic equipment maintenance shop will contain a radio-frequency interference screen room. The screen room shall have a minimum floor area of 150 ft^2 (13.9 m^2) and a minimum of 60dB attenuation of electromagnetic radiation from 100 kHz to 100 MHz. All shielding shall conform to MIL-STD-188/124. Any deviation from these requirements will be contained in the BESEP.

8.3.3.5 Disconnects. Safety disconnect switches shall be provided at the rear of each transmitter power amplifier. Where plenum chambers are used, the disconnect shall be inside the plenum near the rear of the transmitter.

8.3.3.6 Circuit Breakers. Separate circuit breakers for the exciter of each transmitter shall be installed at the technical power panel.

8.3.3.7 No-Break Power. Class D no-break power will normally not be provided for a transmitter building.

8.3.3.8 Emergency Power. Emergency power normally is required.

8.3.3.9 Grounding Provide secure grounds for equipment, buildings, and all electronic systems in accordance with MIL-STD-188/124 and MIL-HDBK-419.

8.3.3.10 Bonding

          a) Transmitters shall be bonded to the equipotential plane via the shortest available route.

          b) Metal objects in the building, including structural steel, reinforcing steel, flashing, downspouts, gutters, cable trays, pipes, and ventilators, shall be electrically bonded unless otherwise specified in the BESEP.

          c) Isolated metal items not exceeding 2 feet (0.61 m) in any direction may be considered for bonding on a case-by-case basis.

          d) Reinforcing steel shall be bonded together at a maximum spacing of 8 feet (1.44 m) on centers or as set forth in the BESEP.

8.4   Receiver Buildings. The receiver station contains a number of antennas for detecting a variety of radio frequencies from distant transmitters. Receiver buildings house the radio receivers and related electronic equipment, as well as computers for storing and/or transmitting received communications to the communication center via microwave or wire circuit. For further information, refer to NAVELEX 0101,102. See Figure 13 for a typical building layout.

8.4.1   Architectural and Structural. In addition to the requirements of Section 3, receiver buildings are generally one story, but a second story will be required when a Naval Security Group department is included. Details will be set forth in the BESEP.

8.4.2   Mechanical. Computing, receiving, and other electronic equipment housed in receiver buildings generally requires close year-round temperature and humidity control. Refer to Section 4 and the project BESEP for specific requirements.

8.4.3   Electrical

8.4.3.1   Lighting. Fluorescent lighting may be used in receiver buildings when they are equipped with integral radio-frequency interference filters.

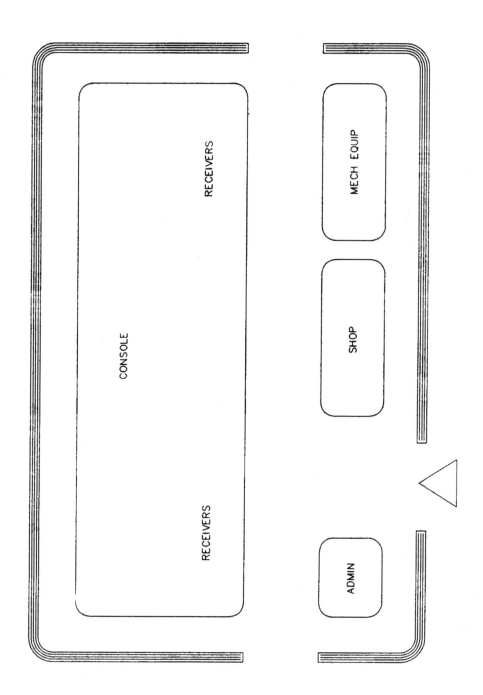

Figure 13
Functional Layout Typical Receiver Building

The power line filters shall comply with the requirements for conducted electromagnetic interference of Class A3 equipment, Test CE03.

8.4.3.2   Interference Suppression. All electrical and mechanical equipment that generates radio-frequency interference shall be equipped with suppression and shielding to eliminate such interference.

8.4.3.3   Cable Vaults. Cables shall be brought into the building through a cable vault, either above or below ground.

8.4.3.4   Cable Trays. Provisions shall be made for installation of cable trays as required by the BESEP.

8.4.3.5   Bonding

        a) Reinforcing steel shall be bonded together at a maximum spacing of 8 feet (1.44 m) on centers or as set forth in the BESEP.

        b) The bonding of metal objects, including structural steel, reinforcing steel, flashing, downspouts, gutters, cable trays, pipes, and ventilators, shall be provided only as set forth in the BESEP.

8.4.3.6   Grounding. Grounding shall include the bonding of all grounding electrodes associated with electric wiring systems, telephone, lightning protection, and piping systems which enter the building. Refer to MIL-HDBK 419 Vol. II, section 1.6.

8.4.3.7   Shielding. The criteria for transmitter facilities shall apply.

8.4.3.8   Emergency Power. Class D & C power is normally required.

8.5   Direction-Finder Facilities. The pusher Direction-Finder (DF) unit determines the origin of a high-frequency transmitted radio signal by means of a cross-fix between two or more DF facilities. Pusher units and other arrays less costly to construct generally will be used in lieu of Wullenweber DF arrays; however, because Wullenweber DF arrays have performance advantages over the smaller arrays, they may be used where performance is the overriding consideration.

8.5.1   Architectural and Structural. In addition to the requirements in Section 3, acoustical treatment of NAVSECGRU elements shall provide noise attenuation within the area to a level commensurate with its use. (See NAVFAC DM-1.03) Treatment measures for floors, ceilings, and walls will be specified in the BESEP, along with any special requirements.

8.5.2   Mechanical and Electrical. The criteria for radio receiver buildings are usually applicable. Any deviations will be set forth in the BESEP.

8.6   Command/Control/Intelligence Centers. Command/control/intelligence centers normally include administrative space, digital computer systems, interactive terminals, graphic display systems, closed-circuit television systems, secure briefing areas, and extensive external and internal communication capabilities supported by wire lines. Essentially, design criteria applicable to communication centers and digital computer facilities apply to command/control/intelligence centers. Specific guidance concerning the layout of the facility, physical security requirements, and types of systems will be set forth in the BESEP.

8.6.1   Architectural and Structural-. Special requirements shall be as set forth in the BESEP.

8.6.2   Mechanical. Special requirements shall be as set forth in the BESEP.

8.6.3   Electrical. Special requirements shall be set forth in the BESEP

8.6.3.1   Emergency Power. Normally, UPS and emergency power are required.

8.7   Training Facilities. The mission of an electronic training facility is to provide an environment similar or identical to that of an operational site. The facility should provide individuals and teams with theoretical and hands-on training, so that trainees may become proficient in equipment operation and maintenance. A realistic man-machine interface environment is critical to ensure successful personnel performance in tactical environments. The typical electronic training facility should include equipment such as transmitters, receivers, and computers which are identical to those currently in use. The specific design requirements will be set forth by the user operational command. For further information, refer to NAVELEX 0101,109, Naval Training Facilities.

8.7.1   Architectural and Structural

8.7.1.1   Configuration. The design should be flexible to allow for future expansion and/or adaptation of the space for different training programs. The following are among the factors to be considered:

a) Individual study areas;

b) Peak demand plumbing design;

c) Mailrooms;

d) Corridors adequate for class movement;

e) Facilities for off-hours duty personnel;

f) Data center;

g) Administrative spaces for instructors;

h) Adequate floor-to-ceiling heights for raised floors, cabling, ceilings, lights, raceways, ducts, etc.

i) Dummy loads, interface devices, and simulators;

j) Simulated shipboard environments.

8.7.1.2 <u>Floors</u>. Live loads should be calculated using a realistic estimate of occupancy. Mechanical, telephone, and radio equipment rooms, radio receiving rooms,, terminal equipment rooms, and equipment-supporting roof areas should use 150 pounds per square foot (psf).

8.7.1.3 <u>Partitions</u>. Movable and relocatable partitions will be required in all non-bearing applications.

8.7.1.4 <u>Flooring</u>. Raised flooring provides maximum flexibility and should be used in lieu of trenching wherever practical.

8.7.2 <u>Mechanical</u>

8.7.2.1 <u>Electronic Shipboard Equipment</u>. Much of the electronic equipment installed in training facilities is a replica of that used aboard ship. Typically, that equipment is water-cooled rather than air-cooled. The project BESEP must be consulted for the required information.

8.7.2.2 <u>Non-Shipboard Electronic Equipment</u>. Mechanical requirements for non-shipboard electronic gear are given in Section 4.

8.7.3 <u>Electrical</u>

8.7.3.1 <u>Power Requirements</u>. In most situations, the determination of power requirements is straightforward. Usual power requirements are as follows:

a) Audiovisual remote control devices at lecterns;

b) Banked lighting with door and lectern control centers;

c) Central service cores to serve two or more classrooms;

d) Electrical services located so as not to interfere with movable walls;

e) Service to accommodate training aids;

f) Open or closed-circuit television systems, including studio and viewing areas.

8.7.3.2 <u>Emergency Power</u>. Unless specified in the authorizing document, emergency and no-break power shall not be provided.

8.7.3.3 <u>Grounding</u>

a) The green-wire grounding system specified in NFPA 70 shall be used in every shore training facility.

b) Consider supplemental grounding accommodations in accordance with MIL-STD-188/124 and MIL-HDBK-419, as required for each case.

c) Red/black criteria and methodology shall be as delineated in Chapter 12 of NAVELEX 0101,102, and MIL-HDBK-419.

8.7.3.4 Shielding

a) Where there is a great deal of DC signaling, such as in computer, CIC-mockup, and simulation areas, consider provisions for coaxial cable to prevent signal interaction.

b) Shielded enclosures or rooms lined with foil or mesh shall be used where low-noise and/or low-level devices must be aligned or demonstrated.

8.7.3.5 Electromagnetic Compatibility (EMC). Since the training equipment must be capable of operation in various stages of disassembly, the shore training facility must compensate for electromagnetic-field retention deficiencies in the training equipment.

a) Effective grounding systems for EMC shall be developed as required for the individual case.

b) The training-equipment station ground shall be isolated from all other ground systems in the facility,

c) Each classroom shall have a separate, AWG 4/0 (or larger) insulated ground feeder.

d) Each piece of equipment, sub-assembly, test fixture, and test equipment shall be connected to the station ground feeder. The AC green-wire protective ground shall not be used as a substitute.

e) Transmitters, exciters, and power amplifiers shall terminate in well-shielded, impedance-matched dummy loads.

f) The transmission line to each dummy load shall be well shielded and as short as possible.

8.8 Naval Air Station Control Towers. The primary function of the control tower is to centralize control over aircraft activities, both on the ground and in the air, and to promote safe and orderly movement of air traffic. The Visual Flight Rules (VFR) room is housed at the most advantageous position and elevation with respect to the airfields to provide complete visual control. The tower receives support from the Instrument Flight Rules (IFR) room, which provides radar contact at distances beyond visual range and under other than optimal visual conditions. The tower includes space on various floors for electronic Air Traffic Control (ATC) equipment, in addition to facilities within the tower cab for control and operation of the equipment. The control tower structure also provides space for passageways for interconnecting cables. For further information, refer to NAVELEX 0101,107.

8.8.1 Architectural and Structural. In addition to the general requirements of Section 3, the control tower shall conform to the following:

The standard control tower includes a control room (control cab), electronic equipment rooms, an emergency communication systems, emergency generator equipment, air conditioning equipment, and sanitary facilities. It is normally a five-story structure, although control towers may contain as many as ten stories to provide adequate visibility. A height of 43 feet (13.11 m) from the ground to the floor of the control cab is the minimum acceptable elevation. The standard air station control tower is usually an integral part of the operations building. If the control tower is a separate unit, the design should allow for future expansion of the operations building. The ground floor area should be large enough to permit easy repair and maintenance of the emergency generator. The electronic equipment room should be designed to house the emergency communication equipment, voice recorders, the main distribution frame, and other equipment. The use of FAA standardized designs for control towers is recommended.

8.8.2   Mechanical. The requirements of Section 4 apply to the mechanical design of control towers, except as follows. Consult the project BESEP for additional guidance.

        a) Remote transmitters and receivers associated with towers generally require air conditioning.

        b) If remote buildings are associated with the towers, a central alarm system should be provided for fire, equipment failure, and other out-of-tolerance conditions, such as high temperature.

        c) Special fire protection requirements may exist for remote buildings.

8.8.3   Electrical

8.8.3.1   Power Requirements. The primary power source shall be used during normal operating conditions. An automatic-start and switchover emergency generator shall be located on the ground floor. Unless an automatic-start generator is immediately available, battery-operated equipment is required.

8.8.3.2   Lighting Requirements

        a) Ceiling. Ceiling lights shall be recessed so as not to reflect in the windows of the cab.

        b) Console. Low-intensity directional lighting shielded from the equipment operator's direct view shall be provided on top of consoles for nighttime operation. The light shall be directed along the planes of the console work surfaces with a minimum of window reflections.

        c) Floor. Low-level lights shall be provided under consoles for nighttime operation to allow safe movement about the cab without reflections.

        d) Intensity control. All lighting for administrative work, operation of controls, and instrument reading shall be compatible with installed equipment and shall have adjustable intensity controls.

8.8.3.3   <u>Alarm Requirements</u>. As a minimum, alarms shall be provided to indicate loss of power, loss of air conditioning, and fire.

8.8.3.4   <u>Cabling</u>

a) Cable vault. Cables shall enter the control tower through a cable vault. This area shall be devoted to organizing and routing cables prior to their entry into the cable shaft.

b) Cable shaft. Power and communication cables from the adjacent building shall pass through a utility duct and enter the cable vault below grade. From the cable vault, the cables shall pass through a vertical tunnel called a cable shaft. Shaft access off a tower stair landing shall be provided at least every 15 feet (4.6 m).

c) Junction room. The junction room is the primary access area to the control cab floor. The control consoles shall open into this space. Power and control cables pertinent to the control cab's function shall converge here and be terminated or rerouted, and the communication, control, and power feeder ducts shall branch here.

d) Interior wiring. Cable shall be run in the spaces provided by standard cellular floor construction.

8.8.4   <u>Communications</u>. The quantity and type of communication equipment will be set forth in the BESEP. As a minimum, a normal system and an emergency system will be required.

8.8.4.1   <u>Normal Communication System</u>. This system consists of HF and VHF/UHF radio equipment as required by the operational mission of the air station. This includes any communication control console equipment, ancillary equipment, and any standby or backup equipment.

a) Standby equipment. Standby radio equipment is tuned to the frequency of the primary equipment, and any filaments are kept hot, so it can be put into operation with no warm-up period. Upon failure of the primary equipment, transfer to the standby equipment is effected instantly by pressing a button on a console.

(b) Backup equipment. Backup equipment may be of the same type as the primary and standby equipment, but it is not necessarily tuned to the same frequency, and it is not kept hot.

8.8.4.2   <u>Emergency Communication System</u>. A minimum capability system, used only when the normal system is inoperative, keeps the station in limited operation by diverting air traffic, landing only aircraft that cannot be diverted to another airfield. This system shall be completely independent of the normal system. Control of the emergency communication system shall be completely independent of normal console control facilities.

8.8.4.3   <u>Grounding</u>. Criteria for transmitter and receiver facilities shall apply.

8.8.4.4 <u>Suppression</u>. Electronic noise suppression and elimination of interference shall be provided as set forth in the BESEP.

8.9 <u>Satellite Communication Ground Stations.</u> A Satellite Communication (SATCOM) ground station transmits and receives Radio Frequency (RF) signals to and from a satellite in a fixed geosynchronous orbit. This system provides communications for large areas of the world using only one satellite. A typical SATCOM ground station contains one or more large, rotating, dish-type antennas equipped with a sensitive RF receiver and transmitter. The site usually contains buildings and/or transportables to house the RF equipment. For further information, refer to NAVELEX 0101,105, <u>Satellite Communication System</u>. Figure 14 shows the functional layout of a typical ground station.

8.9.1 <u>Architectural and Structural</u>

8.9.1.1 <u>Configuration</u>. The operations building shall contain an equipment maintenance area. The building shall also house emergency generating equipment and power conditioning equipment. Pad and building layout will be indicated by the BESEP.

8.9.1.2 <u>Antenna Pad</u>. The pad adjacent to the building shall be reinforced concrete and shall provide for radome installation when required. Hardstands will also be required when transportable equipment is provided.

8.9.1.3 <u>Floors</u>. Raised flooring shall be provided for the fixed plant. Flooring systems shall consist of 1-1/2 inch (38.1 mm) stringer widths, and panels shall be 24 inches (0.61 m) square.

8.9.2 <u>Mechanical</u>. Much of the electronic equipment associated with satellite communications is provided by the satellite agency. It may differ from the electronic equipment in other Naval facilities, in that it normally requires direct duct connections to the air conditioning equipment instead of using room air for cooling. Consult the BESEP for guidance.

Other requirements of Section 4 shall apply to the mechanical design for satellite communication equipment.

8.9.3 <u>Electrical</u>

8.9.3.1 <u>Power Requirements</u>. Primary and secondary power sources may be either base-generated or commercial, but they shall be separate, reliable sources. Emergency power for use during primary and secondary power outages shall be provided by means of an emergency generator. No-break power shall be provided as set forth in the BESEP.

8.9.3.2. <u>Lighting</u>. Fluorescent lighting with approved RF filters may be used in all areas, except inside the radome and in the immediate vicinity of the antenna.

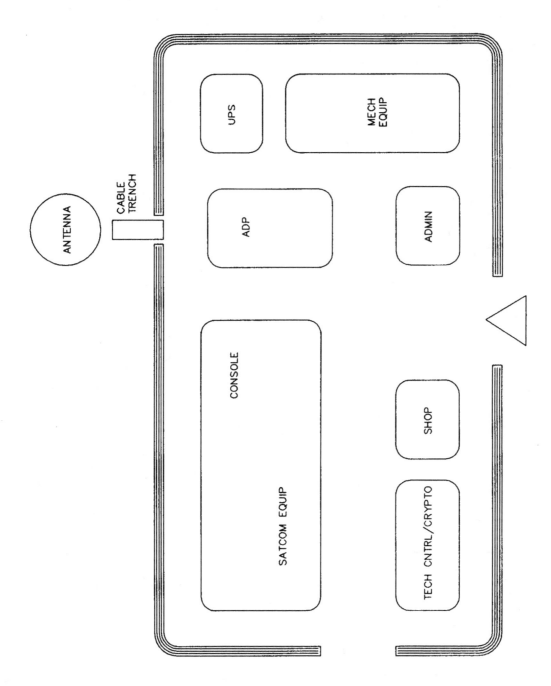

Figure 14
Functional Layout Typical SATCOM Ground Station

8.9.3.3   Cabling

a) Cabling from the pedestal to the building shall be run in a cable trench, as set forth in the BESEP.

b) Transmission and communication lines shall enter the building through an underground cable vault.

c) Cabling within the building shall be run in overhead cable trays as set forth in the BESEP.

d) Where red/black security conditions exist, the installation shall conform to MIL-HDBK-419.

8.9.3.4   Interference Suppression. The criteria for receiver facilities shall apply.

8.9.3.5   Grounding

a) Hardstands require grounding and shall be part of the equipotential plane specified in the BESEP.

b) Antenna grounding shall be as set forth in the BESEP.

c) Where radomes are required, a properly grounded lightning rod shall be installed at the top of the radome.

d) Where red/black security conditions exist, the installation shall conform to MIL-HDBK-419.

8.10   Transportables

8.10.1   Description. Transportable facilities are electronics equipment enclosures that range in size and construction from small tactical enclosures that can be carried within or towed behind a truck to large semi-permanent enclosures that are essentially assembled and completed in the field. The main transportable classifications are as follows:

8.10.1.1   Transportable/tactical. This is an enclosure that can be transported by standard military means, quickly placed in operation, and easily relocated. The electronic equipment must be built in to the greatest extent possible so that the system can be activated by opening protective doors/covers and applying power to quick disconnect fittings. Wheels and leveling jacks or skids may be provided.

8.10.1.2   Transportable/relocatable. This is an enclosure that can be completed, with all equipment installed, checked out, and secured, prior to shipment. The enclosure, if possible, should conform to the dimensions of International Organization for Standardization (ISO) containers, in accordance with OPNAVINST 4620.8, Use of Internal Containers, Special Purpose Vans, and Tactical Shelters. These units require minimal assembly and hook-up in the field. These transportables are generally much larger and heavier than tactical units, and offer more flexibility. in electronic and environmental control system layout and design. The enclosures are usually mounted on leveling jacks or stands, or they may be mounted on a field-constructed foundation.

Where ISO units cannot be used such as 10 foot wide units, built-in tension members in the wall and built-in spreader bars in the roof should be provided so roof line hoist points can be used at the quarter points of the container. Removable end panels, some with personnel doors, are often times provided to simplify the installation and removal of equipment. Flexible (accordion like) weather covers and demountable walkways are used to connect the transportable either to a building or to other transportables when applicable. When stair access is provided allow sufficient platform space at the top for door swing and so it will not be necessary to back down the stairs to open the door. Railings should meet OSHA 2201, Safety Standards for General Industry.

8.10.1.3 Transportable/non-relocatable. With this type of enclosure, there is little or no emphasis on relocatability. Shipment may include any number of packages, which are field-assembled and installed. Factory fabrication and pre-assembly are usually limited to providing several large portions of the enclosure or complex, along with some portions of the power wiring, plumbing, and air conditioning. The enclosures are usually mounted on field-supplied foundations or supports.

8.10.1.4 Sub-categories. Various sub-categories of transportables include trailers, semi-trailers, vans, milvans, containers, and shelters. These are generally in the tactical or relocatable category, but, in certain applications, could be classified as non-relocatable. Containers are ISO standard-sized units. Two are of particular interest for housing and transporting Naval electronic equipment; both are 8 feet (2.4 m) wide by 8.5 feet (2.6 m) high, and are either 20 feet (6.1 m) or 40 feet (12.2 m) in length. These units are designed for a gross weight of 44,800 pounds (20 317 kg) and 67,200 pounds (30,475 kg), respectively, and are provided with rugged corner fittings for hoisting, stacking, and shipping. Milvans (the Army equivalent of ISO containers) are only available in the 20-foot (6.1 m) version. Shelters are tactical units and rarely exceed 7 feet (2.1 m) wide by 7 feet (2.1 m) high by 12 feet (3.7 m) long. Trailer, semi-trailer, and van dimensions depend on the particular vehicle selected for use. For further information, refer to NAVELEX 0101,110, Installation Standards and Practices. Figure 15 shows a typical transportable installation.

8.10.2 Architectural and Structural

8.10.2.1 Structural Requirements. Transportable facilities shall be designed to withstand equipment weights and other in-service loads, plus any load resulting from storage, handling, and transportation. Where possible, the design should incorporate the longeron/stressed skin (semi-monocoque) concept. This permits maximum interior space with respect to outside dimensions, but limits the size and location of openings and requires careful design of framing around opening. (In extreme cases, an entire wall or end may be open where one container is coupled to another, and it may be necessary to use shipping panels that provide structural support at the openings when the containers are in transit.)

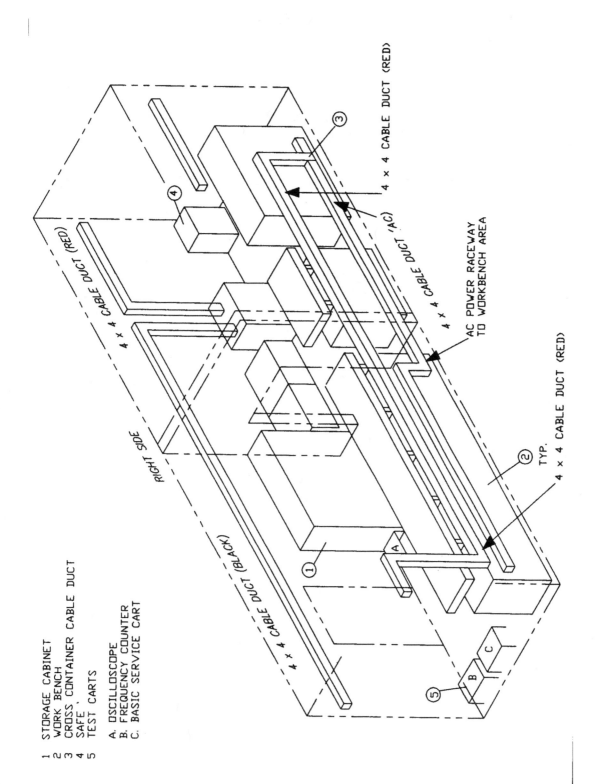

1 STORAGE CABINET
2 WORK BENCH
3 CROSS CONTAINER CABLE DUCT
4 SAFE
5 TEST CARTS

A. OSCILLOSCOPE
B. FREQUENCY COUNTER
C. BASIC SERVICE CART

Figure 15
Typical Transportable Installation

a) Strength, weight, corrosion resistance, shielding, Radio-Frequency Interference (RFI) attenuation, equipment mounting requirements, fire criteria, and compatibility of dissimilar metals shall be considered when selecting frame and skin materials. Container framing may be formed, rolled, or extruded sections of aluminum or steel. Interior and exterior skins are often of aluminum since it is lightweight and corrosion-resistant and provides a significant amount of RFI protection even if RFI gasketing and cut-off cores are not provided. Any of several plastics may be used as a skin material for applications such as radar windows; steel may be used if adequate finishes are applied.

b) Flooring shall be aluminum plate or plywood-metal lamination, so that metal surface is exposed top and bottom. Vinyl tile is typically added to the top surface.

c) Between interior and exterior wall skins, a thermal barrier, such as wood or thermosetting plastic laminate conforming to National Electrical Manufacturers Association (NEMA) Grade L or LE, is required. Any remaining space in the wall shall be filled with fiberglass or polyurethane insulation.

d) Roof construction shall be similar to wall construction, except that the exterior skin shall be a single sheet of aluminum alloy laminated to a hardboard backing to resist stresses from personnel walking on the roof, as well as transportation-related stresses. The laminating adhesive shall be flexible to allow for thermal expansion of the roof sheet.

8.10.2.2 **Weather Resistance**. Exterior surfaces of the container shall be as airtight and watertight as possible. Water vapor passing through any opening or non-vaporproof barrier in the outer shell will condense in the insulation or in cavities in the insulation space. As a result, the thermal conductivity of the insulation may be much higher than its original value, so that required interior conditions are not achieved or a much greater load is placed on the equipment.

a) Some moisture may enter the space by diffusion through cracks or permeable surfaces. The major amount, however, is brought in by infiltration.

Because of the difficulty of making the outer skin completely leakproof, additional protection is necessary. Three methods are possible:

(1) using foamed-in-place plastic insulation,

(2) lining the inside of the exterior skin with a non-permeable vapor barrier, such as aluminum foil, coated with a plastic binder that can be sealed at the joints, or

(3) coating the interior surface of the exterior skin with vapor-sealing compound. Care in installation is important, especially around wiring, piping, and framing. The use of the first method is encouraged.

b) The interior skin should be as vaportight as practicable. It must be water-resistant so that cleaning does not readily soak the insulation.

c) All doors shall fit properly and shall be gasketed to minimize air and heat leakage. Hardware for doors shall withstand the severe conditions that may be encountered.

8.10.2.3 Finishes. Floor surfaces shall be of wood or metal. If floors are wood, they shall be metal-faced plywood with the edges well sealed against water penetration. Metal floors shall be watertight. Floors shall be covered with vinyl tile for ease of cleaning. Metal-faced plywood, aluminum, certain plastics, and other materials are suitable for interior wall surfaces. Unless the exposed surface is metallic, the material shall have a flame spread classification not greater than 22.8 or a smoke developed rating not greater than 50, in accordance with UL Standard 723-1983, Test for Surface Burning Characteristics of Building Materials. Glass-reinforced plastic materials have been used for interior and exterior wall surfaces and, commercially, several manufacturers now produce all-plastic containers. Where there is a need for radar transparency, a thermosetting plastic exterior panel may be used, provided it is painted to match the surrounding surfaces with special radar-transparent paint. Where walls must be used to support equipment for other loads, vinylized metal-clad plywood should be considered. These panels are metal-clad on both sides but vinylized on the interior exposed side only.

8.10.2.4 Equipment Layout. Equipment layout shall be as specified in the BESEP.

8.10.3 Mechanical. The general requirements of section 4 apply to the design of transportables. Deviations and additional requirements are listed below.

8.10.3.1 Tactical Transportables. Tactical transportables impose severe limitations on the mechanical equipment.

a) Air Conditioning. Air conditioning equipment must be small and rugged. Generally customized, direct-expansion, air-cooled, through-wall units using refrigerant R12 are provided, even though size and weight limitations make them inefficient and expensive in comparison with standard commercial units. Refrigerant R12 is preferred to R22 because of the high internal pressure generated by R22 at storage temperatures encountered during transportation. Also, commercial units normally are rated at 90 degrees F (32 degrees C) dry bulb and 75 degrees F (24 degrees C) wet bulb. These factors preclude the use of most small commercial units currently available.

b) Backup Air Conditioning. Each unit shall be equipped with two increments of cooling, each sized for half the design load; a third increment shall be provided for the evaporator coil strictly for use as standby. This requires a special evaporator coil circuited to achieve proper load balance with any two increments operating.

c) Heating. Normally, electric strip heaters are provided with the air conditioning units and mounted downstream of the evaporator coil. Heaters may be used for dehumidification,, but should be controlled not to operate whenever there is a full cooling load. Provisions for backup heat are not required.

8.10.3.2 <u>Relocatable and Non-Relocatable Transportables</u>. Relocatable and non-relocatable transportables more closely resemble permanent facilities than tactical ones. Therefore, mechanical design is not as restricted, and the general guidelines listed in Section 4 are more appropriate.

a) Air Conditioning. Tactical types air conditioners are inappropriate for this class of transportables, but R12 refrigerant should be used, since refrigerant storage pressures during transportation would be excessive with R22. Various types of systems may be used, including split systems with remote DX condensers, commercial-quality single package DX units, and chilled-water systems with air-cooled chillers. Chilled water systems are applicable to groups to transportables, especially if they are non-relocatable.

b) Backup Air Conditioning. This is required for any function specified as critical in the project BESEP. Special circuiting of coils is not required. It is recommended that units be incremented to handle only a portion of the load, with an extra unit used for backup.

c) Heating. Normally, the heat load is minimal and heat required to maintain space conditions should be provided as part of the air conditioning unit. Electric resistance heating is preferred because of its simplicity and reliability. Backup heating is not required.

8.10.4 <u>Electrical</u>. In most cases, the requirements for transportables are similar to those for transmitter and receiver buildings. In all cases, installation shall be in accordance with NFPA 70.

8.10.4.1 <u>Conductors</u>

a) Stranded Conductor. Stranded cable shall be used whenever possible. The use of stranded conductor is mandatory for all power wiring.

b) Solid Conductor. In non-power applications where solid conductor must be used, the conductor shall be securely anchored along the entire run, and sufficient slack shall be incorporated at termination points to compensate for in-transit motion.

8.10.4.2 <u>Conductor Installation</u>

a) Maintainability and future expansion requirements are prime design considerations.

b) Cabling and wiring shall be installed to permit circuit checking or circuit renewal without removing major pieces of equipment. Planned wiring and preformed harnesses shall be incorporated wherever possible.

c) Wires and cables shall be situated to minimize inductive and capacitive effects.

d) Connector plugs and receptacles shall be positioned to facilitate rapid connection and disconnection of major items.

e) Wire and cables shall be long enough to allow otherwise inaccessible equipment to be removed for service without disconnection.

f) Conductors shall have sufficient clearance from high-heat-radiating components.

g) The minimum bending radius shall not be violated in any case.

8.10.4.3 Metallic Ducts

a) Ducting is the preferred method of running cable.

b) Under-floor areas shall be used for cabling only if the under-floor structure is specially designed for this purpose.

c) Conduit shall be used where penetration of walls, floors, or roofs is necessary.

8.10.4.4 Conductor Terminations

a) Terminal Boards; Wires and cables shall be arranged on terminal boards to minimize inductive and capacitive effects.

b) Distribution Frames. All cables, except antenna cable carrying information to or from equipment, cabinets, or containers, shall terminate at a distribution frame or junction box. Audio and control circuit terminations shall be separate to minimize interference.

c) Terminations. Terminals that grip the wire insulation shall be used. To facilitate equipment removal, quick-disconnect cable terminations are desirable.

d) Insulation Protection. Textile and glass-insulated ends of wire shall be secured against fraying by mechanical means or by applying varnish conforming to military specifications.

e) Strain Relief. Strain relief shall be provided such that, when portable cables are plugged into container-mounted connectors, the weight of the cable does not hang on the connector.

f) Service Loops. Sufficient slack shall be left in conductors to make at least two additional terminations.

g) Spare Conductor Runs. Ten percent spares shall be available so that conductors may be replaced without having to run new cables. Spares shall be long enough to reach the remote terminal within the cabinet or equipment; they shall be folded back and laced until used.

h) Antenna Cables. Where control and signal cables leading to antennas penetrate the roof of a van or other similar transportable, a suitable protective cover shall be provided.

8.10.4.5 <u>Power Requirements</u>

a) Primary Power. Relocatable and non-relocatable installations shall be designed to operate on commercial power or generator power, with the determining factors being the availability, accessibility, and reliability of commercial power at the site. Tactical installations usually require portable generators.

b) Emergency Power. The need for emergency power shall be considered for each case.

c) Power Connections. The installation of power connections for transportable installations is NAVFAC's responsibility.

8.10.4.6 <u>Lighting</u>. The primary lighting system shall be designed to operate off the primary power source. Battery-operated emergency lighting shall be provided for use during primary power outages.

8.10.4.7 <u>Bonding</u>. The criteria governing permanent electronic facilities are applicable to the design of transportables. Specific requirements include:

a) Direct Bonds. Soldering and welding are the preferred methods. Where semi-permanent bolted bonds are required, lock washers of the internal-external type shall be used.

b) Indirect Bonds. Low-inductance bonding straps shall be used. The strap ends shall be brazed or silver-soldered to the ground bus or terminal. The connections to the equipment or cabinets shall be bolted and shall have a measured resistance of 0.01 ohms or less.

8.10.4.8 <u>Grounding</u>. The criteria governing permanent electronic facilities are applicable to the design of transportables. Specific requirements include:

a) Relocatable and non-relocatable. Grounding techniques shall be of the more permanent type, since the facility, one installed, will operate for an indefinite period. If the facility is moved, the grounding system essentially will be abandoned in place.

b) Tactical. The ground system shall be designed such that the facility is capable of carrying the majority of its ground rods and interconnecting cables.

c) Responsibilities. The grounding facilities at installations where transportable configurations are used shall be designed by NAVFAC and installed by Public Works or contractor personnel responsible for constructing entire facility. The electronic equipment installer shall tie into the ground stub with a short connection from the container.

8.10.4.9 <u>Shielding</u>. Shielding shall be used as required for the individual case. Where shielding is used, the criteria governing permanent electronic facilities shall be observed.

8.11 <u>Automatic Data Processing Centers</u>. The automatic data processing (ADP) center provides computer-oriented information processing and display systems. The ADP center support all Naval Shore systems and assigned ship systems in all matters requiring digital, stored-program computers. In addition to computers, the ADP center contains the peripheral devices required to form a complete system. Its functions include processing, displaying, and transmitting data for data collection, data distribution, inquiry processing, computer time-sharing, and message switching. Details of system needs will be set forth in a BESEP, or by the user command. For further information, refer to NAVELEX 0101,111, <u>Digital Computer Systems. Vol I of II</u>.

8.11.1 <u>Architectural and Structural</u>. In addition to the general requirements of Section 3, data processing facilities shall comply with the following:

8.11.1.1 <u>Configuration</u>. In addition to the computer room, the data processing center shall include a data storage room a data base office, a tape/disk library, keypunch room office space, and a production control room. The design should provide for future expansion.

8.11.1.2 <u>Floors</u>. Raised floors shall be used in computer areas.

8.11.2 <u>Mechanical</u>. Basic design criteria are provided in Section 4. The criteria in this paragraph are directed toward larger computer facilities classified as data processing centers. Although the criteria primarily apply to areas housing the computing equipment, ancillary spaces, including storage areas for magnetic disks and tapes, punch cards, and paper require similar environmental control. Tolerances for ancillary areas are wider, however, and environmental control system reliability is not as critical.

8.11.2.1 <u>Design Criteria</u>. Most manufacturers recommend that the computers use room air for cooling. Normally, a room condition of 72 $\pm$ 2 degrees F (22.2 $\pm$ 1 degrees C) and 45 $\pm$ 5 percent RH is provided where the latent/sensible ratio of the load requirement matches that of the coil performance giving the optimum economic performance. Some manufacturers, however, require that cooling air be introduced directly to the machine. Generally, this requires a supply air temperature of about 65 degrees F (18 degrees C) and a relative humidity of 40 to 65 percent to avoid condensation within the equipment. This will in turn require that reheat tempering of the supply air is necessary. This can double the required cooling capacity, unless waste heat is used for the purpose and is not a recommended design.

8.11.2.2 <u>Cooling Loads</u>. Information on the heat release of the computing equipment must be obtained from the BESEP or from the computer manufacturer. Because of the relatively low occupancy and the small percentage of outside air, heat gains in computer rooms are almost entirely sensible. As a result of this and the low room design conditions, the air circulation rate per ton of cooling normally must be higher than the circulation rate for comfort cooling. The high rate of heat release from computer results in a high load density, yielding ratios of 50 to 75 square feet per ton of cooling. Computer areas are therefore susceptible to drafts if care is not taken in the layout of supply registers and diffusers. Hot spots can also occur because of the concentrated loads.

8.11.2.3 Air Conditioning Systems. Systems serving data processing centers should be independent of other systems in the building if the building central system is secured during the winter season. Chilled water systems may be cross-connected to provide backup. The air conditioning systems available for use are listed in Section 4. They may be classified as self-contained units (using air or water for condensing), decentralized air-handling equipment, and central systems.

a) Self-contained Units. Units are completely packaged, with reciprocating compressors and refrigerant coil, filters, humidifiers, provisions for a reheat coil, operating controls, and instrumentation such as signal lights, dirty filter alarms, and other status/alarm lights. Construction of major items should be corrosion-resistant. Units can be arranged to supply air down into a floor plenum or up to overhead ducts and/or a plenum with diffusers. The units are located in the spaces served, and are provided with water-cooled condensers connected to a remote cooling tower, water-to-air heat exchanger, or other heat rejection device. Multiple units are usually provided, and the outdoor ventilation air is normally introduced through one of them.

b) Decentralized Air-handling Units. These are similar to self-contained units, but are served by remotely located refrigeration equipment, usually through chilled water coil connections. This arrangement is appropriate in facilities where both air-cooled computing equipment and water-cooled equipment (such as computers associated with simulators) is installed. Chilled water normally should be in the range of 47 to 50 degrees F (8.3 to 9.4 degrees C) to provide the high sensible cooling ration required in computer areas. This type of system requires central chiller equipment capable of 24- hour-per-day, year-round operation.

c) Central Systems. These have an advantage in that no computer room floor space is taken up by the air-handling units, and all servicing and maintenance takes place outside the computer rooms. Central systems must be designed, however, to accommodate future expansion of the computer space or changes in loads, and are not as widely used as the other systems.

8.11.2.4 Supply Air Distribution. As indicated in Section 4, air distribution is important in all electronic equipment areas. Data processing centers impose even more stringent requirements to accommodate load changes and future expansion, with minimal changes to the mechanical equipment. Under-floor or ceiling plenum supply is commonly used to provide the required flexibility.

a) Under-floor Systems. Where raised floors are provided, it is often advantageous to use them as a supply plenum for conditioned air. If air must be introduced directly to the machine, more stringent restrictions are imposed on allowable temperature and relative humidity than if it were introduced to the room; this approach should therefore be used only if required by the equipment. When the plenum supplies air to the room, relocatable floor panels with registers or perforated flush panels are used. The perforated panels are suitable for high-traffic areas and may be located close to the equipment, since they produce a high degree of mixing with room air. Floor registers are not flush and should not be located in areas of heavy traffic or where wheeled carts are expected to operate. They are capable of longer throw and better directional control and may be appropriate for use in certain locations.

b) Above-ceiling Systems. Overhead supply systems through ceiling plenums with perforated panels as diffusers are occasionally used for computer rooms. This can cause hot spots in high-load areas, however, and generally is not as flexible as diffuser grille distribution. An advantage of ceiling systems is that they do not collect dirt from the floor area. Best conditions are usually achieved by distribution ductwork, with the air discharged into the space through diffusers in the ceiling. Perforated ceiling tiles are usually inadequate as air outlets for final distribution to a computer room, since they normally are incapable of handling the large quantities of air required in these applications.

Return air may also be ducted from ceiling-mounted return air registers in an overhead system. Short-circuiting between supply and return may occur if care is not exercised in locating the supply and return terminals. Overhead ducted supply usually serves normal building loads for lights, occupancy, and the structure, while under-floor systems normally serve to augment the central system in removing heat from the computers. Either can be used, but both may create drafts, especially when ceilings are low. With both systems, provisions must be made to maintain room relative humidity.

8.11.2.5 Computer Equipment Cooling. Some computer equipment requires distilled water for cooling. This requirement will be indicated in the BESEP. Normally, when this requirement exists, the cooling system is provided by the manufacturer as part of the computer equipment, and is connected to a heat exchanger, which in turn can be connected to the chilled-water systems as a final heat sink. Chiller water piping, therefore, is often required in the computer room. Careful installation of the piping and proper insulation, where necessary, should minimize the possibility of leaks and condensation. A separate refrigeration system for the computer equipment is desirable because of the need for continuous year-round operation, the need for higher reliability than with comfort applications, and the need for some components (in critical applications) to be on the UPS circuit. Heavy loads such as chillers or compressors are never to be placed on the UPS output circuit. Some installations require the chilled water system to be sized for growth so that it can be expanded to accommodate future additions to the data processing center.

8.11.2.6 Condensing Methods. In some locations, cooling towers may be acceptable; in others, the need for winterization and excessive water treatment may preclude their use. Air-cooled refrigeration condensers with head pressure controls and separate hot gas and liquid lines for each, refrigeration circuit are widely used. In installations where multiple refrigeration systems are involved and/or the units are remote from the point of heat rejection, air-cooled heat exchanger systems tend to simplify the piping and controls. Glycol-loop exchangers (or water-loop exchangers in climates not subject to freezing) permit use of a closed water system connected to the condenser and facilitate compressor head pressure control by pressure-actuated water regulators at the condenser.

8.11.2.7 Instrumentation. Most automatic data processing centers require room temperature/humidity recording devices. Alarms should be incorporated with the recorders to signal if temperature or humidity is too high or two low. In large rooms, recorders should be installed in each zone. When chiller water is supplied directly to the computer, records of chilled water inlet and outlet temperatures and pressures should be maintained. Sensing devices to indicate the presence of water in the computer room under-floor cavity are desirable if chilled water piping is installed in the cavity. All monitoring and alarm devices should provide local indication, and, if a central monitoring and control point exists, the alarms should be transmitted to that location.

8.11.2.8 Fire Protection. As a minimum, smoke detectors should be provided in both the room and the air conditioned air stream. Under raised floors, these devices should be provided in the cavity, regardless of whether it is used as a plenum, when electrical cabling is installed, The fire protection system should include a controlled and properly sequenced shutdown of computer power, either manual or automatic, depending on its criticality and the potential for false alarms. Refer to MIL-HDBK-1008 for additional guidance.

8.11.3 Electrical

8.11.3.1 Lighting

     a) Fixtures. Lighting fixtures shall be recessed within the ceiling where possible. Fixtures extending below the ceiling shall not interfere with equipment installation.

     b) Sunlight. Direct sunlight shall not interfere with the low levels of illumination needed for visibility of the console and signal lamps.

     c) Control. Lights for general illumination shall be sectionally controlled by switches so that portions of the lighting can be turned off as desired.

     d) Emergency Lights. Emergency lighting shall be provided as required by NFPA 101, Code for Safety to Life from Fire in Buildings and Structures. The lighting shall be adequate to light the computer area when general illumination is off. In transportables, provisions shall be made to keep emergency lights from operating during shipment.

8.11.3.2 Power Requirements. Design shall conform to Article 645 of NFPA 70.

     a) Equipment Power. The designer shall comply with the power requirements and characteristics peculiar to each piece of computer equipment. The information will be supplied by the BESEP or the user command.

b) Secure Power. Power used to supply equipment that processes red information may require special service to ensure security. The BESEP will set forth all such requirements.

c) Frequency Conversion. Where frequency conversion is required, either a motor generator or static converter shall be used. Motor generators shall be located in a room separate from computer equipment. Static converters can be located in the computer room if they are adequately grounded to prevent EMI. Situations where two converters are required will be indicated in the BESEP.

d) Emergency Power. Class C auxiliary power, when required, will be specified in the BESEP.

e) No-break Power. Class D auxiliary power is normally required and shall be as set forth in the BESEP.

f) Convenience Outlets. Convenience outlets in ADP equipment units shall be run off the technical bus. Additional outlets shall be provided at 12 to 14 foot (3.66 to 4.27 m) intervals around the perimeter of the room. These outlets shall be run off the non-technical bus.

8.11.3.3 Power Distribution

a) Bus Configuration. Power shall be distributed in a split bus system, with one bus serving the technical load and one bus serving the non-technical load.

b) Technical Bus. The technical bus shall serve the computer equipment and minimal lighting.

c) Non-technical Bus. The non-technical bus shall serve all other power requirements.

8.11.3.4 Power Control

a) Main Disconnect. The "emergency off" switch shall be as close to the main exit as possible.

b) Emergency Power Monitoring System Controls. When an emergency power system is required, a facility monitoring panel shall be provided in the computer room and electrical equipment room. The panel shall indicate when emergency power is in use (emergency power on), sound an alarm with a manual shut-off feature (emergency power alarm), and provide telephone communication between the computer room and the alternate power supply.

8.11.3.5 Grounding

a) Equipment Protection. Equipment shall be grounded in accordance with manufacturer's specification and comply with MIL-STD-188/124 and MIL-HDBK-419.

b) HEMP Protection. When such protection is required, the criteria will be found in MIL-HDBK-1012/2 and the BESEP.

8.11.3.6 <u>Bonding</u>. Bonds between cabinet chassis and the raised floor shall not exceed a design goal specified resistance of 5 milliohms.

8.11.3.7 <u>Shielding</u>

a) Shielding shall be provided as needed for each case.

b) Shielding for red information areas shall be as set forth in the BESEP.

8.12 <u>Oceanographic Facilities</u>. Oceanographic Centers process signals from underwater areas via submarine cables (commonly referred to as sea cables) to a shore processing facility. The shore equipment is normally located in a Terminal Equipment (TE) building. Specific guidance concerning the layout of the facility, physical security requirements, and types of systems will be set forth in the BESEP. The TE building may also contain administrative offices and electronic power generation equipment.

8.12.1 <u>Architectural and Structural</u>. The facility shall comply with the general requirements of Section 3. Special requirements shall be as set forth in the BESEP.

8.12.2 <u>Mechanical</u>. Basic design criteria are provided in Section 4. Special requirements shall be as set forth in the BESEP.

8.12.3 <u>Electrical</u>

8.12.3.1 <u>Underwater Cable</u>. Typically, one or more buried cables run from the sea to the TE building. The signals on these cables are extremely sensitive to interference from nearby AC power circuits and strong RF fields. No electric conductors, equipment, facilities or structures of any kind shall be installed in the vicinity of these cables. A set of guidelines for installations in the vicinity of underwater cables is given below. Written permission from the SPAWAR (PMW-180) is required, on a case-by-case basis, to grant waivers from these guidelines.

8.12.3.2 <u>Quiet Zones</u>. Quiet zones for a typical site are defined in Figure 16.

a) Quiet Zone A shall be kept completely free of AC power circuits.

b) No structures or facilities of any kind shall be installed in Quiet Zone B except as specifically noted below. This restriction specifically includes antennas of any kind, overhead or buried communication lines, and AC power lines.

(1) AC-powered security lights may be installed in Quiet Zone B provided they are designed to prevent the injection of power-line frequency currents into the earth in the quiet zone. Isolation transformers and ground

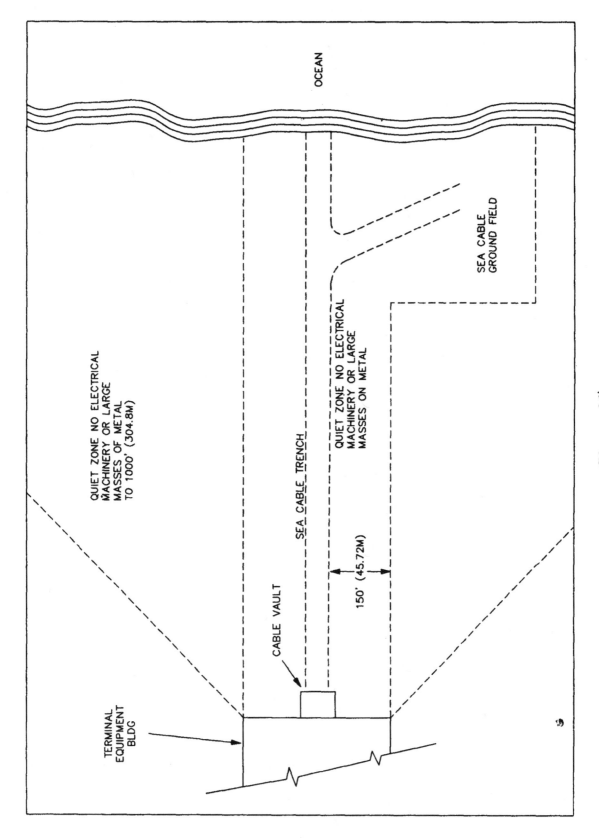

Figure 16
Sea Cable Clearances

fault current interrupters are required for security lights in the Quiet Zone. Safety ground leads associated with these circuits must not be connected to local earth grounds at individual fixtures. Non-conducting supports are recommended. If conducting supports are used, individual isolation transformers are required at each fixture to isolate safety and local grounds.

(2) Electrical security devices, energized entirely from remote direct current sources, may be used in Quiet Zone B provided they are not grounded to local grounds within the quiet zone.

(3) Guy wires terminated in Quiet Zone B are required to have at least one insulator in each individual wire.

(4) A three dimensional clearance of at least 25 feet must be maintained between the sea cable and any current-carrying conductors installed in Quiet Zone B. Conductors crossing the cable path must be routed at right angles to the cable for at least 25 feet on each side. Conductor paths parallel to the cable shall be avoided. Any such conductors are required to have two adjacent return conductors in the same cable arranged so as to cancel magnetic fields. Overhead installations are preferable to buried installations anywhere in the quiet zone.

(5) Security fences within Quiet Zone B are required to be grounded and bonded as specified in para. 5.5.3.3. Fences crossing the cable path must run at right angles to the cable for a distance of at least 25 feet on each side of the cable. Care shall be exercised in placing fence posts on any similar structures requiring excavation in quiet zones A or B.

8.12.3.3 <u>Grounding</u>. Special grounding plans, tailored to each site, are required for oceanographic facilities and will be included in the BESEP where appropriate. Complete isolation of signal, safety, and neutral grounds is required except at specifically designated points.

a) All sites have main ground identified as the G2 ground. In addition, some sites have special grounds (G1 and G3) which are directly associated with underwater cables and are installed and maintained by underwater cable installation organizations. G2 grounds normally consist of multiple driven electrodes with a measured resistance of less than one ohm. G2 ground field construction details are included in the BESEP where appropriate.

b) The G2 ground field is connected to a main G2 ground plate by a single, large (typically 750,000 circular mils) conductor. No other connections to this ground field are authorized without specific written permission from SPAWAR (PMW 180).

c) The main G2 ground plate is connected to a number of branch ground plates dedicated to individual subsystems. One branch ground plate is dedicated to safety grounds, building frame grounds, and power circuit neutral ground connections. Other branches are connected to specific subsystems as specified in the BESEP. These grounding systems are in accordance with Volume 2, para. 1.4.3 of MIL-HDBK-419 and NFPA 70, Article 250.

d) The neutral conductors for all supplementary power sources, such as generators and isolation transformers and as defined in NFPA 70, Section 250-5(d), are required to be grounded to the G2 power and frame ground plate. NFPA 70, Section 250-91(C) permits additional grounds. These additional neutral grounds must be connected to the same point on the neutral as the G2 ground connection.

e) Three-phase delta-wye isolation transformers are required at most sites to eliminate objectionable ground currents. In many cases this function can be combined with voltage-stepdown requirement. These transformers will be specified in the BESEP. Since the purpose of these transformers would be defeated by interconnecting primary and secondary neutrals, it is required that only three wires <u>(no neutral wire)</u> be run from the source to the primary windings. A single new neutral and safety ground is required to be established by connecting the secondary neutral directly to the G2 power and frame ground plate in accordance with NFPA 70, Sections 250-23(a) and 250-26(a). Electrostatic shields in isolation transformers must be connected to the source safety ground lead and not directly to either neutral. Insulated conduit bushings are required to isolate source and load safety grounds.

8.12.3.4 <u>Power Sources.</u> The technical power distribution systems for oceanographic facilities were designed to be supplied from redundant technical power busses energized by continuously-running diesel engine-driven alternators. These busses provide an essentially continuous source of well-regulated power and only stable loads are permitted. Specifically, cyclic loads are not permitted on busses serving technical equipment. Non-technical or commercial power sources were used for technical power only in emergency or otherwise exceptional circumstances. As a conservation measure, these sites are being converted to use commercial power continuously with engine alternators used only for emergency power as described in Section 5.3.

Emergency power sources are required to be able to support each site continuously and indefinitely. This requirement plus the need for separating technical and cyclic loads means that at least three engine alternators are normally required at each site. UPS Systems are required to filter commercial power and support critical loads during transitions to and from emergency power. Figure 5 shows the typical power plant and distribution system required. Any site specific requirements shall be stated in the BESEP.

a) Load requirements are contained in the BESEP and are normally stated in terms of the existing maximum demand load and the anticipated future demand load for each of the components of the operational load as defined in Section 5.3(b). These loads are normally given in volt-amperes. A power factor of 0.85 is normally assumed for technical load power calculations.

b) Installed power capacity requirements are based on the total known future load requirements plus a nominal 25 percent allowance for unanticipated growth.

c) Steady-state load voltage requirements are normally 120/208V plus or minus 3 percent at the technical equipment input terminals. Transient excursions must not exceed plus or minus 5 percent from any point within the plus or minus 3 percent steady-state band and must not persist for more than one second.

d) Technical power is required at 60Hz with a steady-state tolerance of plus or minus 1/4 percent. Transient frequency deviations of plus or minus 1 percent from any point within the plus or minus 1/4 percent steady-state band are permitted for up to one second.

e) Rotary frequency converters are normally provided when only 50 Hz commercial power is available. The use of 50 to 60 Hz UPS equipment for this function is not recommended unless an adequate continuous source of 60 Hz bypass power can be provided.

f) Certain sites require 400 Hz power in addition to the normal 60 Hz power. This power is normally provided by means of either rotary or solid state 60 to 400 Hz frequency converters as specified in the BESEP. Power to drive these converters is normally included in the critical technical load requirements.

8.12.3.5 <u>UPS Requirements</u>. UPS systems are used at oceanographic facilities to provide a source of continuous high quality power for critical technical loads and to provide a transition power source when switching to/from commercial power and emergency power. An UPS provides continuous output power by using energy from a set of storage batteries. These batteries are rated in terms of the length of time they can support the full UPS load before becoming discharged. UPS batteries are recharged automatically when AC power is available and battery charging power must be included in UPS input power estimates. UPS batteries at oceanographic facilities are required to be sized to supply the full rated UPS load for a minimum of 15 minutes.

Section 9: ANTENNA SYSTEMS

9.1   General. The design of antennas involves three basic
considerations: siting, arrangement and selection of types of antennas and
circuitry, and structural supports. Requirements for siting, separation and
spacing, types of antennas, circuitry, grounding systems, and propagation are
normally determined by NAVELEX. Refer to Section 1 of this manual for
information on procedures and responsibilities.

9.2   Site Consideration. For information concerning site
considerations, refer to NAVELEX 0101,103; NAVELEX 0101,104; and NAVELEX
0101,113.

9.3   Design Criteria

9.3.1   Structural. Antenna supporting structures shall conform to the
NAVFAC DM-2 Series, Structural Engineering. Special criteria, such as
deflection and twist limitations for supports, shall be as specified in the
BESEP. Wind load shall be calculated using the basic design loads from MIL-
HDBK-1012/2 with no increase in the basic allowable unit stresses. Towers 300
feet (91.44 m) or less in height may be designed in accordance with Electronic
Industries Association (EIA) Standard RS-222-C, Structural Standards for Steel
Antenna Towers and Antenna Supporting Structures; design of towers greater
than 300 feet (91.44 m) may conform to this standard when it does not conflict
with more stringent requirements in MIL-HDBK-1002/3, Steel Structures and
NAVFAC DM-7 Series, Soils and Foundations, or the BESEP.

     All structural steel towers used as vertical radiators shall be
galvanized. Galvanizing should be considered for other structural steel at
locations where difficult access, height, limitations on interruption of
service, or similar conditions make periodic painting or maintenance
difficult. To minimize distortion, assemblies to be galvanized shall be
designed in accordance with the provisions of The Design of Products To Be Hot
Dip Galvanized After Fabrication, a publication of the American Hot Dip
Galvanizers Association.

9.3.2   Foundations. Foundations for antenna supporting structures shall
be designed in accordance with the requirements of NAVFAC DM-2 series and
NAVFAC DM-7 Series. Foundation design shall take into consideration antenna
erection procedures, as well as reactions due to service loads. Some typical
antenna erection procedures are outlined in NAVELEX 0101,104.

9.3.3   Appurtenances

9.3.3.1. Guys. Structural design of guys shall conform to the MIL-HDBK-
1002/3. Detrimental effects of guys on antenna operating efficiency shall be
minimized in accordance with NAVELEX 0101,104. Turnbuckles, adjustable
sockets, or other take-up means shall be used at the lower ends of all guys.

9.3.3.2 Insulators

a) Guy insulators. Types, ratings, numbers, and spacing of guy insulators are specified in the BESEP or set forth by the command responsible for the design of the antenna.

b) Base insulators. Types and ratings of base insulators are specified in the BESEP or set forth by the command responsible for the design of the antenna.

9.3.3.3 <u>Ladders and Platforms</u>. For essential details pertaining to ladders, lubber-loops, safety cages, platforms, railings, safety chains, and similar appurtenances, refer to MIL-HDBK-1001/2. Ladders, ladder bars, or step bolts shall be placed on pole supports or along one leg of tower framing, except where electronic considerations prohibit use of metal in or near supports. Where feasible, rest platforms shall be provided on towers, preferably at intervals not exceeding 100 feet (30.5 m).

9.3.3.4 <u>Fencing</u>. For details, refer to Section 6 of this handbook.

9.3.3.5 <u>Lighting and Marking</u>. Lighting and marking of antennas and antenna supports shall conform to FAA Advisory Circular AC 70/7460, <u>Obstruction Marking and Lighting</u>. For further information, refer to Section 7 of this handbook.

9.3.3.6 <u>Antenna Pads</u>. Consideration should be given to placing paved pads at the bases of large antennas.

9.3.3.7 <u>Lightning Protection</u>. Lightning protection shall be provided in the form of grounding, surge suppressor and/or sparkgaps. The working voltage and limitations for setting the spark gap will be provided by the user command.

9.3.4 <u>Power Requirements</u>

9.3.4.1 <u>Exterior Power</u>. Some antennas require power for operation of de-icing equipment, rotation devices, and obstruction lights.

9.3.4.2 <u>Cabling</u>. Exterior power cables shall be run underground to the antenna via cable trenches.

9.4 <u>Helix House</u>. The helix house normally supports an LF antenna; it is a copper-lined building which houses the antenna tuning and loading coils and other components used to match the output impedance of the transmitter to the antenna impedance. The transmitter termination and the antenna termination are also located in the helix house. The transmission system between the transmitter and the helix house depends on the location and number of antenna feeds and/or down-leads required.

9.4.1 <u>Siting</u>. The helix house is usually located at the base of the antenna.

9.4.2 <u>Components</u>. The matching components generally consist of the helix, variometer (variable inductor), and shunt variometer, but some sites use direct series link coupling from the antenna series variometers to the power amplifiers.

9.4.3   Bushings. Feed-through bushings couple the helix house outputs to the antenna down-leads. The bushings are usually gas-filled to reduce the size of the insulator for a given flashover rating. The gas feed line to the bushing shall be 3/8 inch (9.4 mm) or greater in diameter. Details will be set forth in the BESEP.

9.4.4   Shielding. To reduce losses into surrounding materials, the interior of the room containing the tuning coils is shielded. The entire interior, including floor, trenches, walls, and ceiling, shall be lined with copper or its equivalent in aluminum. Doors shall also be covered. Seams and joints shall be continuously brazed or soldered for copper and welded for aluminum. The shielding shall be bonded to the building ground system. Because of the high RF induction heating capability of the signal, no magnetic material should be used inside the shield. Any ferrous material used shall be shielded, and the shield shall be grounded. Shielding thickness shall be provided in the BESEP.

9.4.5   Bonding. For 50-kilowatt helix houses, reinforcing steel shall be welded at joints between longitudinal and transverse rods, along lines 10 feet (3.05 m) apart both ways, forming buses that are carried and grounded to the buried ground system surrounding the helix house. When transmitters are more than 50 kilowatts, reinforcing steel in walls and ceilings shall be welded at every joint where transverse rods pass longitudinal rods.

9.4.6   Safety. Entrance to the helix house shall be restricted during system operation by an interlocked, non-magnetic metallic barrier bonded to the ground system.

9.4.7   Cabling. Transmission lines may be run above ground or underground. Direct burial is preferred, where practical, to protect cables and to permit maintenance and/or security vehicular traffic on the antenna field.

9.4.8   Lighting. Incandescent light fixtures shall be installed on the bulkhead, 8 feet (2.44 m) above the floor.

THIS PAGE INTENTIONALLY LEFT BLANK

Section 10: TRANSMISSION LINES

10.1   General. The type of transmission line chosen for a particular application depends primarily upon the operating power level, characteristic impedance, line losses, and susceptibility to RFI. The three basic types of transmission lines are balances lines, unbalanced lines and waveguides. For detailed discussions, refer to NAVELEX 0101,110.

10.2   Balanced Transmission Lines. Balanced lines consist of two separate conductors operated at equal and opposite potentials. Open-wire lines provide good balance, constant characteristic impedance, and low loss, and they are capable of handling very high power levels. This is particularly true when unusually long distances between the transmitter and antenna are necessary. For a detailed discussion of the physical and electrical characteristics of balanced transmission lines, refer to NAVELEX 0101,104 and NAVFAC DM-4.07, Wire Communication and Signal Systems.

10.3   Unbalanced Transmission Lines. Coaxial cables used in HF transmitter and receiver installations operate with the center conductor at some potential other than ground and the shield (outer conductor) at ground potential; they are therefore called unbalanced transmission lines. Coaxial transmission lines are used almost exclusively at all receiving installations, as well as in most transmitting applications. For a detailed discussion of the physical and electrical characteristics of unbalanced transmission lines, refer to NAVELEX 0101,104. For cable selection, environmental considerations, insulation and sheath, and types of wire and cable, refer to NAVELEX 0101,110.

10.4   Waveguides. A waveguide is a transmission line consisting of a dielectric medium through which electromagnetic waves propagate. Waveguides are generally distinguished by the frequency of the electromagnetic radiation they transmit.

10.4.1   Microwave Waveguides. The three types of microwave waveguides are rectangular, circular, and elliptical. For detailed discussions, refer to NAVELEX 0110,110.

10.4.2   Optical Waveguides (Fiber Optics). Optical fiber cables offer several advantages over cables with metallic electrical conductors and metallic waveguides. The optical fiber cable provides a non-conductive dielectric media as the transmission medium; this results in electrical isolation between the transmitter and the receiver. Optical 'energy is unaffected by other forms of electromagnetic radiation; therefore, optical fiber cables can operate in a noisier electrical environment. Optical energy is guided within the fiber; crosstalk inherent in cables with metallic electrical conductors is extremely low in optical fibers because of the stronger guidance of the media. Optical fiber cables are smaller and lighter than electrical cables of the same transmission capacity. The advantages of fiber optic cables over copper-based systems in general include lower attenuation, larger bandwidth, higher security, and the absence of electromagnetic interference, shock hazards, and short circuits. Their importance depends on the requirements of the system under consideration. See Section 7 for safety considerations when using fiber optics.

10.4.2.1 <u>Cable Structures</u>. In general, the same types of sheathing used with copper-based systems can be used with glass-based systems. The systems may include aerial cables, submerged cables, rodent-resistant cables, and other types of cables. There is a lack of standardization in the area of cable sheath design, but as the technology matures, standardization undoubtedly will take place.

10.4.2.2 <u>Cable Selection</u>. The most important mechanical features to consider in selecting a cable are as follows:

    a) Tensile strength;

    b) Adequate strength-member selection;

    c) Bending radius;

    d) Support requirements;

    e) Environmental specifications;

    f) Length of continuous run available;

    g) Lengths that can be safely pulled in conduits and raceways;

    h) Probability of fiber breakage;

    i) Compression strength.

        Cables designed to contain electrical conductors and optical fibers are also feasible and generally available. For example, twisted-pair wires can be included for signaling applications, or to carry electrical power to optical repeaters along the cable route.

10.4.2.3 <u>Optical Connectors</u>. The method used for splicing lengths of fiber to each other and to terminating the ends in the appropriate connectors is an important part of the optical link. Both fiber splices and cable terminations can cause significant power losses and add to the complexity and cost of the installation. The lack of standardization is also a problem in the technology of optical connectors. In general, it can be assumed that a good fiber optic connector will not have an attenuation greater than 1.5 dB. This number is typical, but should be updated to the current state of the art at the time of installation. The associated cable strength-member tie-off and sheathing termination is characteristic of the cable type and is not different from similar copper-based cables.

10.4.2.4 <u>Fiber Splices</u>. Optical fibers can be spliced in two ways: by fusion and by an adhesive index-matching material. These two techniques typically exhibit equal losses, varying from 0.1 to 0.5 dB optical attenuation; however, in the current state of the art, the optical quality of the index-matching adhesive (usually an epoxy) may deteriorate with time. Fusion, on the other hand, is performed by melting the optical fibers together into one mechanically and optically continuous fiber. Tool kits are readily available to implement either of these techniques.

10.4.2.5 Components of a Fiber Optic System. A fiber optic system contains three major components: the light source, which may be an Injection Laser Diode (ILD) or a Light Emitting Diode (LED); the light detector, which may be an Avalanche Photodiode Detector (APD) or a P-I-N diode; and the transmission medium, the optical fiber cable.

        a) Light source. Injection laser diodes provide greater power output and a narrower spectral bandwidth of light than LEDs, enabling more power to be coupled into the optical fiber and providing greater transmission capacity or bandwidth. ILDs are not linear, which limits their capacity to transmit analog channels. ILDs are generally used in digital systems. LEDs become attractive when bandwidth requirements and the system length permit; they are lower in cost, operate over a wider temperature range, have a longer expected life, and offer greater long-term stability.

        b) Light detectors. APDs improve receiver sensitivity by approximately 10 dB or more over P-I-N detectors, since they provide internal gain. APDs, however, require an auxiliary power supply, introduce more noise, and are more costly than P-I-N detectors. The system requirements will dictate the choice of detector.

        c) Light transmission. In any material, light travels at a speed characteristic of the material and lower than the speed of light in free space. The ratio of the speed in the material to the speed in free space defines the refractive index of the material. When light traveling in one medium encounters another material of lower refractive index, the light is bent towards the material of higher refractive index.

        If the angle of incidence is increased sufficiently, the bent light will travel along the interface of the materials. This angle is known as the critical angle. At an angle greater than the critical angle, the light will be totally reflected from the interface and follow the transmission path. (See Figure 17.)

        d) Transmission medium. An uncabled optical fiber consists of a core, a cladding, and a protective coating. The core material has a higher index of refraction than the cladding material, and therefore light tends to be confined within it. The core material can be plastic or glass, although glass provides lower attenuation and greater bandwidth performance. The cladding material may be air (although this is not practical), plastic, or glass; glass provides greater stability and compatibility with the core glass. To confine the injected light to the core, the angles of reflection of propagating ray must exceed the critical angle. This reflection angle is unique to each mode and determines the length of the path associated with each mode. The result is that each mode progates at a characteristic axial velocity, so that dispersion limits the maximum rate at which information can be transmitted.

        Multi-mode fibers, where the change in refractive index from the core to the cladding is a discrete step, are called step index fibers. Typically, their bandwidth is limited to approximately 30 MHz per km. (See Figure 17.) Since light travels faster in a material with a lower refractive index, fibers with cores whose index of refraction is high at the center, but

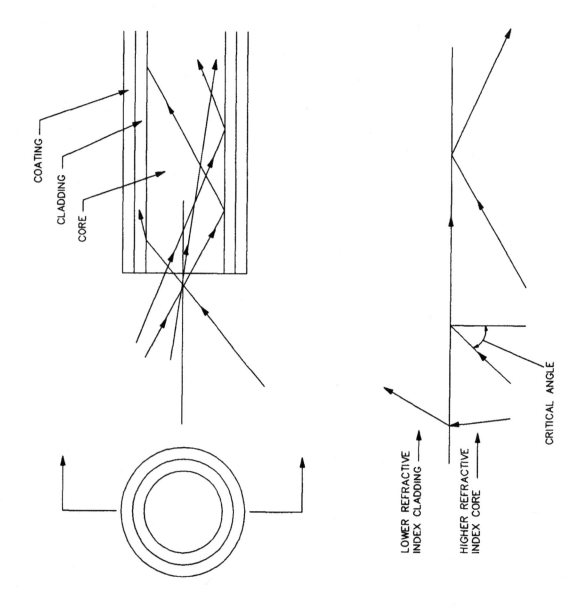

Figure 17

Ray Trace Diagram of Light Entering a Step Index Fiber

decreases in a parabolic profile to the value of the cladding index at the core/cladding interface, are generally available. This type of fiber is called graded index fiber and provides band-widths greater than 1 GHz. (See Figure 18.)

e) The parameters affecting the transmission characteristics of optical cables are attenuation, pulse dispersion, and numerical aperture. Attenuation is a measure of the light loss (signal loss) per unit length of transmission medium and is designated in decibels of optical power lost per kilometer (dB/km). The losses result from absorption (due to impurities in the glass), scattering (due to density fluctuations in the glass), and radiation losses (due to microbending of the glass). Attenuation is inversely proportional to temperature change.

Pulse dispersion (also called pulse spreading) is the measure of the spreading or broadening of the light signal (pulse) and is designated in nanoseconds per kilometer (ns/km). The spreading results from material dispersion (due to the spectral width of the light source) and modal dispersion (due to the slightly different velocities for each optical mode present). Consequently, pulse spreading is a function of the path length. The bandwidth can be calculated from the pulse dispersion and is given in MHz-km. Numerical Aperture (NA) is a measure of the light-collecting capability of an optical fiber and is a function of the difference in the refractive indices of the fiber core and cladding. A large NA permits more light to enter the fiber.

f) Cable installation criteria. Fiber optic cables are similar to conventional cables in terms of the handling and installation procedures required. The limiting tensile load varies from manufacturer to manufacturer and among different cable types of a given manufacturer. The tensile load typically found is in excess of 300 pounds; therefore, many conventional installation tools and procedures can be adapted to optical cable. A few essential differences must be recognized, however, to ensure a successful installation. Glass, although an intrinsically strong material, is relatively brittle. As a consequence, it is important to monitor and control the cable-pulling force during installation. Unlike copper conductors, which can stretch up to 20 percent before breaking, glass fibers Can only be strained 1 to 2 percent before breaking.

Another important factor is that fiber optic cables have a minimal bend radius, generally 10 times larger than the cable diameter. This is not unlike metal-base cables of the same bandwidth capability. Considerable attention should be given to determining the correct lengths of cable to order and install. The objective should be to determine the cable segment lengths required for the installation without exceeding maximum recommended tensile load and-to permit cable splicings and connectorization as required.

g) System design. Design of an optical fiber link occurs at two levels. First, the individual components must be designed or specified, and then their interaction must be considered in a system-level design. The design goal of a communication link is to transfer information from one point to another without degradation. For analog systems, this means designing for a desired Signal-to-Noise Ratio (SNR), bandwidth, and distortion level. In

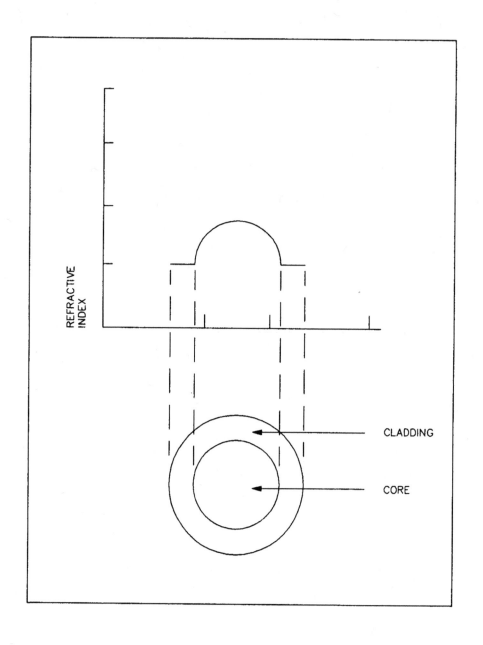

Figure 18
Graded Index Fiber

the present state of the art, analytical expressions for signal distortion in optical sources are not available; but even though distortion effects can not be considered in minute detail, they can be measured and specified independently. SNR and bandwidth analyses can be performed. For digital systems, the design goals are specified in terms of Bit Error Rate (BER) and bandwidth. For both types of systems, calculations that pertain to the overall SNR or BER performance can be performed. To summarize the interactions between modules, a system link budget should be prepared.

h) <u>Link budget</u>. To determine whether or not the system has adequate optical power to meet the design goals for SNR or BER, the engineer can use a link budget. The link budget starts with the total source power. All of the system losses (the input coupling losses) are listed, along with the received optical power. The difference between the losses and the received power required to meet the SNR or BER design goals is the power margin available for system degradation. A sample link budget is shown below:

LINK BUDGET

Available Power Source	_____mW	_____	dBm
Input Coupling Loss		_____	dBm
Fiber Loss		_____	dBm
Splice Loss		_____	dBm
Connector Loss		_____	dBm
Output Coupling Loss		_____	dBm
Receiver Power	_____mW	_____	dBm
<div align="center">Target BER</div>			
Required Receiver Power	_____mW	_____	**dB**
Margin		_____	**dB**

i) <u>System bandwidth calculation</u>. The designer must be aware of the overall system bandwidth to ensure that his design goal has been met. This is particularly true in analog systems. The main concern is that selection of the wrong fiber can lead to bandwidth limitations. (It is assumed that bandwidth concerns have been accounted for in the transmitter and receiver designs.) The calculation can be performed by first taking the square root of the sum of the squares of the individual module rise times:

EQUATION:

$$t_{r_t} = [(t_{r_{Tx}})^2 + (t_{r_f})^2 + (t_{r_{Rx}})^2]^{0.5}$$

(3)

Where:

t_{r_t} is the total system rise time

$t_{r_{Tx}}$ is the light output rise time from the transmitter,

t_{r_f} is the rise time of the fiber

$t_{r_{Rx}}$ is the receiver rise time

The overall system bandwidth f_{3dB_t} is then calculated using the standard relation:

$$f_{3dB_t} = 0.35/t_{r_t}$$

Where:

f_{3dB_t} = overall system bandwidth

10.5   <u>Structural Supports For Open-Wire Lines</u>. Structural supports for open-wire transmission lines shall be as specified for antenna supports (Section 9 of this manual), with the following modifications:

10.5.1.   <u>Design Loadings</u>. In determining design loadings, consider the possibility of all transmission wires on one side of a support being broken with wind and ice loading.

10.5.2   <u>Deflection Limitations</u>. Deflection limitations do not normally apply to supports for transmission lines.

10.6   <u>Responsibilities</u>. Transmission lines will be specified either in the BESEP or by the manufacturer.

BIBLIOGRAPHY

American National Institute, Inc. (ANSI). 1430 Broadway. New York, NY 10018.

A156.2-1976	Locks and Lock Trim
C95.1-1982	Safety Levels with Respect co Human Exposure to Radio Frequency Electronic Fields, 300 KHz to 100 GHz.
C95.2-1982	Radio Frequency Radiation Hazard Warning Symbol.

Federal Specification, available from the Superintendent of Documents, U.S. Government Printing Officer, Washington, D.C. 20402.

AA-D-600B	Door, Vault, Security
FF-H-106	Hardware, Builders', Locks and Door Trim, General Specification for
FF-H-116	Hinges, Hardware, Builders'
FF-H-121	Hardware, Builders', Door Closers

Industrial Laminated Thermosetting Products; NEMA Standard LI 1-1971 (R1976), National Electrical Manufacturers Association, 2101 "L" Street, N.W., Washington, DC 20037.

Information Gate-keepers, Inc., Brookline, Massachusetts

Design Curves for Optical Waveguide Digital Communication Systems, Vol. 3.

Fiber Optics Design Aid Package, Vol. 4, Parts 1 and 2

Design Handbook for Optical Fiber Systems, Vol 2

Intrusion Detection System, NAVFAC DM 13.02, available from Naval Publications and Forms Center, 5801 Tabor Avenue, Philadelphia, PA 19120.

Life-Cycle Costing Manual for the Federal Energy Management Programs, National Bureau of Standards Handbook 135, December 1980, available from the Superintendent of Documents, U.S. Government Printing Office, Washington, DC 20402.

Locks and Lock Trims, BHMA 601, Builders Hardware Manufacturers Association, Inc., c/o Trade Group Associates, Managers, 60 East 42nd Street, Room 511, New York, NY 10165.

Military Handbook. Standards and Specifications, available from Naval Publications and Forms Center, 5801, Tabor Avenue, Philadelphia, PA 19120. Private individuals and organizations may purchase from the Superintendent of Documents, U.S. Government Printing Office, Washington, D.C. 20420.

MIL-HDBK-1002/5	Timber Structures
MIL-HDBK-1002/6	Aluminum Structures, Composite Structures, Structural Plastics, and Fiber-Reinforced Composites
MIL-L-15596	Lock, Combination (Safe and Safe Locker)

Multi-mode Optical Waveguides with Graded Refractive Index: Theory of Power Launching, P. DiVita and R. Vanucci, No. 11, 2765-2772, Applied Optics, 15 (1976).

National Fire Codes, available from National Fire Protection Association, Batterymarch Park, Quincy, MA 02269

NFPA 255	Standard for Business Materials Test of Surface Burning, Characteristics of

Naval Shore Electronics Criteria, available from Naval Publications and Forms Center, 5801 Tabor Avenue, Philadelphia, PA 19120.

0101,101	General
0101,112	Microwave and Troposcatter Communications Systems
0101,115	Digital Computer Systems, Vol. II of II
0101, Appendix VIII	Handbook of Naval Shore Station Electronics Criteria

NAVFACENGCOM Guide Specification, NFGS-16650 Radio Frequency Interference Power Line Filters, available from the Commanding Officer, Naval Publications and Forms Center, 5801 Tabor Avenue, Philadelphia, PA 19120.

Optical Communications: Devices, Circuits, and Systems, M. J. Howes and D. V. Morgan, from John Wiley & Sons, Inc., New York.

Receiver Designs for Fiber Optic Communications Optimization in Terms of Excess Noise Factors that Depend on Avalanche Gains, Y. Takasaki and M. Maeda, COM-24(1976) No. 12, 13-1346, IEE Transactions on Communications, available from Institute of Electrical and Electronics Engineers, Inc., 345 East 47th Street, New York, NY 10017.

Threshold Limit Values for Chemical Substances and Physical Agents in the Work Environment with Intended Changes for 1982, American Conference of Governmental Industrial Hygienists.

Underwriters Laboratories. Inc., UL 768 Combination Locks, 333 Pfingston Road, Northbrook, IL 60062

Utilization of Optical-Frequency Carriers for Low and Moderate Bandwidth Channels, W. M. Hubbard, Bell System Technical Journal, 52 (1973), No. 5, 731-765.

REFERENCES

NOTE: Unless otherwise specified in the text,
users of this handbook should utilize the latest
revisions of the documents cited herein.

FEDERAL/MILITARY SPECIFICATIONS, STANDARDS, BULLETINS, HANDBOOKS, AND NAVFAC GUIDE SPECIFICATIONS:

The following specifications, standards, and handbooks form a part of this
document to the extent specified herein. Unless otherwise indicated, copies
are available from Commanding Officer, Naval Publications and Forms Center,
ATTENTION: NPODS, 5801 Tabor Avenue, Philadelphia, PA 19120-5099.

SPECIFICATIONS

    FEDERAL

W-L-305	Light Set, General Illumination (Emergency or Auxiliary)
RR-F-191	Fencing Wire (Chain-Link Fabric)

    MILITARY

MIL-F-29046	Flooring, Raised; General Specification for
MIL-P-43607	Padlock, Key Operated, High Security, Shrouded Shackle

STANDARDS

    MILITARY

MIL-STD-188/124	Grounding, Bonding, and Shielding for Common Long Haul/Tactical Communication Systems
MIL-STD-210	Climatic Extremes for Military Equipment
MIL-STD-461	Electromagnetic Emission and Susceptibility Requirements for the Control of Electromagnetic Interference
MIL-STD-882	System Safety Program Requirements
MIL-STD-1425	Safety Design Requirements for Military Lasers and Associated Support Equipment
MIL-STD-1472	Human Engineering Design Criteria for Military Systems, Equipment and Facilities

HANDBOOKS

MIL-HDBK-411 Volume I	Power and Environmental Control for the Physical Plant of DOD Long Haul Communications Power
MIL-HDBK-411 Volume II	Power and Environmental Control for the Physical Plant of DOD Long Haul Communications Environmental Control
MIL-HDBK-419 Volume I	Grounding, Bonding, and Shielding for Electronic Equipments and Facilities, Basic Theory
MIL-HDBK-419 Volume II	Grounding, Bonding, and Shielding for Electronic Equipments and Facilities, Applications
MIL-HDBK-1001/2	Materials and Building Components
MIL-HDBK-1002/3	Steel Structures
MIL-HDBK-1005/8	Domestic Wastewater Control
MIL-HDBK-1008	Fire Protection for Facilities Engineering Design and Construction
MIL-HDBK-1012/2	High Altitude Electromagnetic Pulse Protection
MIL-HDBK-1013/1	Design Guidelines for Physical Security of Fixed Land-Based Facilities
MIL-HDBK-1190	Facility Planning and Design Guide

NAVFAC GUIDE SPECIFICATIONS

NFGS-13093	Radio Frequency Shielded Enclosures, Demountable Type
NFGS-13094	Radio Frequency Shielded Enclosures, Welded Type
NFGS 13947	EMCS, Large System Configuration
NFGS 13948	EMCS, Medium System Configuration
NFGS 13949	EMCS, Small System Configuration
NFGS 13950	EMCS, Micro System Configuration

<u>NAVY MANUALS, DRAWINGS, P-PUBLICATIONS, AND MAINTENANCE OPERATING MANUALS</u>:

Available from Commanding Officer, Naval Publications and Forms Center (NPFC), 5801 Tabor Avenue, Philadelphia, PA 19120-5099. To Or&r these documents: Government agencies must use the Military Standard Requisitioning and Issue Procedure (MILSTRIP); the private sector must write to NPFC, ATTENTION: Cash Sales, Code 1051, 5801 Tabor Avenue, Philadelphia, PA 19120-5099.

DM-1.01	Basic Architectural Requirements and Design Considerations
DM-1.03	Architectural Acoustics
DM-2 Series	Structural Engineering
DM-3 Series	Mechanical Engineering
DM-3.01	Plumbing Systems
DM-3.03	Heating, Ventilating, Air Conditioning and Dehumidifying Systems
DM-4.05	400 Hz Generation and Distribution Systems
DM-4.07	Wire Communication and Signal Systems
DM-4.09	Energy Monitoring and Control Systems
DM-5.03	Drainage Systems
DM-5.5	General Provisions and Geometric Design for Roads, Streets, Walks, and Open Storage Areas
DM-5.12	Fencing, Gates, and Guard Towers
DM-7 Series	Soils and Foundations
DM-7.02	Foundations and Earth Structures
P-89	Engineering Weather Data
P-442	Economic Analysis Handbook

<u>NAVY DEPARTMENTAL INSTRUCTIONS</u>: Available from Commanding Officer, Naval Publications and Forms Center, ATTENTION: Code 3015, 5801 Tabor Avenue, Philadelphia, PA 19120-5099.

NAVELEXINST 5100.12	Navy Laser Hazards Prevention Program
NAVELEXINST 11000.1	The Base Electronic System Engineering Plan (BESEP and Procedure for Utilization of, 21 July 71)

NAVMED P-5055	Radiation Health Protection Manual
NAVMEDCOMINST 6470.2	Laser Radiation Health Hazards
NAVSEA OP3565/ NAVAIR 16-1-529/ NAVELEX 0967-LPO624- 6010 VOL. I	Technical Manual Electromagnetic Radiation Hazards (U)
OPNAVINST 4620.8B	Use of Intermodal Containers, Special Purpose Vans and Tactical Shelters
OPNAVINST 5100.23B	Navy Occupational Safety and Health Program Manual
OPNAVNOTE 5100 SER 45/5u394867 30 JULY 1985	Personnel Protection Policy for Exposure to Radio-Frequency Radiation (RFR)
NAVELEK 0101 Series	Naval Shore Electronics Criteria Manual
NAVELEX 0101,102	Naval Communications Station Design
NAVELEX 0101,103	HF Radio Propagation and Facility Site Selection
NAVELEX 0101,104	HF Radio Antenna Systems
NAVELEX 0101,105	Satellite Communication Systems
NAVELEX 0101,106	Electromagnetic Compatibility and Electromagnetic Radiation Hazards
NAVELEX 0101,107	Naval Aeronautical Facilities
NAVELEX 0101,108	Naval Security Group Elements, Design and Performance
NAVELEX 0101,109	Naval Training Facilities
NAVELEX 0101,110	Installation Standards and Practices
NAVELEX 0101,111	Digital Computer Systems, Vol. I of II
NAVELEX 0101,113	Navy VLF, LF, and MF Communications System
NAVELEX 0101,114	NAVELEX Calibration Program

OTHER GOVERNMENT DOCUMENTS AND PUBLICATIONS:

The following Government documents and publications form a part of this
document to the extent specified herein.

DEFENSE INTELLIGENCE AGENCY

DIAM-50-3-80   Physical Security Standards for Sensitive
                      Compartmented Information Facilities

(Unless otherwise indicated, copies are available from Commander, Navy
Intelligence Command, NIC-31, 4600 Silver Hill Road, Washington, D.C. 20389).

DEPARTMENT OF DEFENSE (DOD)

DOD 4630.7-M   Major Fixed Command, Control and
                     Communications Facilities Power Systems Design
                     Features Manual

(Unless otherwise indicated copies are available from Superintendent of
Documents, U.S. Government Printing Office, Washington, DC 20402).

FEDERAL AVIATION ADMINISTRATION (FAA)

Advisory Circular   Obstruction Marking and Lighting
AC 70/7460-1F

(Unless otherwise indicated copies are available from U.S. Federal Aviation
Administration, Office of Airport Standards (AAS-200) Department of
Transportation, 800 Independence Avenue, S.W., Washington, DC 20591).

NATIONAL SECURITY AGENCY (NSA)

NACSIM 5203   Guidelines for Facility Design and Red/Black
                    Installations

(Unless otherwise indicated copies are available from National Security
Agency, Director, US Navy Communication Security National Systems (CMSC), 3801
Nebraska Avenue, N.W., Washington, DC 20390).

OCCUPATIONAL SAFETY AND HEALTH ADMINISTRATION (OSHA)

1910.23   Standards for General Industry

1926.403   Battery Rooms and Battery Charging

(Unless otherwise indicated copies are available from Superintendant of
Documents, U.S. Government Printing Office, Washington, D.C. 20402).

<u>NON-GOVERNMENT PUBLICATIONS</u>:

The following publications form a part of this document to the extent specified herein. Unless otherwise specified, the issues of the documents which are DOD adopted are those listed in the Department of Defense Index of Specification & Standards (DODISS).

American Hot Dip Galvanizers Association

The Design of Products to be Hot Dip Galvanized After Fabrication

(Unless otherwise indicated copies are available from American Hot Dip Galvanizers Association, 1101 Connecticut Ave., N.W., Washington; DC 20036).

AMERICAN SOCIETY OF HEATING, REFRIGERATING AND AIR CONDITIONING ENGINEERS (ASHRAE)

Test Standard 52-76,   Method of Testing Air-Cleaning Devices Used in General Ventilation for Removing Particulate Matter

ASHRAE Handbook Series

1988 Handbook   Equipment

1987 Handbook   HVAC Systems and Applications

1986 Handbook   Refrigeration Systems and Applications

1985 Handbook   Fundamentals

(Unless otherwise indicated copies are available from, American Society of Heating, Refrigerating and Air Conditioning Engineers, Inc. (ASHRAE), 1791 Tullie Circle, N.E., Atlanta, GA 30329).

ELECTRONICS INDUSTRIES ASSOCIATION (EIA)

EIA Standard RS-222C   Structural Standards for Steel Antenna Towers and Antenna Supporting Structures

(Unless otherwise indicated copies areavailable from the Electronics Industries Association, 2001 Eye Street, N.W., Washington, DC 20006).

INTERNATIONAL ORGANIZATION FOR STANDARDIZATION (ISO)

Standard 669-1976   Freight Containers, External Dimensions, and Ratings

(Unless otherwise indicated copies are available from the International Organization for Standardization (ISO), 1 Rue De Varembe, Case Postale 56, CH 1211, Geneva 20, Switzerland).

ILLUMINATING ENGINEERS SOCIETY (IES)

Lighting Handbook

(Unless otherwise indicated copies are available from the Illuminating Engineers Society (IES), 345 East 47th Street, New York, NY 10017).

NATIONAL FIRE PROTECTION ASSOCIATION

NFPA 70	National Electrical Code
NFPA 72A	Standard for the Installation, Maintenance, and Use of Local Protective Signaling Systems for Guard's Tour, Fire Alarm, and Supervisory Service
NFPA 72E	Standard on Automatic Fire Detectors
NFPA 75	Standard for the Protection of Computer/Data Processing Equipment
NFPA 78	Lightning Protection Code
NFPA 90A	Standard for the Installation of Air Conditioning and Ventilation Systems
NFPA 101	Code for Safety to Life from Fire in Buildings and Structures

(Unless otherwise indicated copies are available from National Fire Protection Association, Batterymarch Park, Quincy, MA 02269).

UNDERWRITERS LABORATORIES, INC. (UL)

UL 723-83	Test for Surface Burning Characteristics of Building Materials

(Unless otherwise indicated copies are available from Underwriters Laboratories, Inc., 333 Pfingston Road, Northbrook, IL 60062).

CUSTODIAN
NAVY - YD

PREPARING ACTIVITY
NAVY - YD

PROJECT NO.
FACR-0363

www.ingramcontent.com/pod-product-compliance
Lightning Source LLC
LaVergne TN
LVHW060144070326

832902LV00018B/2943